SANDRA K. AT

Quick & Easy Strategies for
Close Reading and Writing

■SCHOLASTIC

New York • Toronto • London • Auckland
Sydney • New Delhi • Hong Kong

Editor: Maria L. Chang
Cover design by Tannaz Fassihi
Cover art by Sean McCabe
Interior design by Maria Lilja

Photos ©: cover girl: Steve Debenport/Getty Images; 110 center: Kerryn Parkinson/NORFANZ/Caters News via ZUMA Press; 112 left: Courtesy Dr Holley Moyes; 112 right: Western Michigan University; 114 left: Library of Congress; 114 right: Alpha Stock/Alamy Stock Photo; 132 seahorse: skynesher/iStockphoto; 132 flying fish: swedishmonica/iStockphoto; 132 archerfish: tane-mahuta/iStockphoto. All other photos © Shutterstock.com. Illustrations: 104, 105, 106, 109, 112, 113, 118, 123 John Lund.

ISBN: 978-1-338-18834-9
Scholastic Inc., 557 Broadway, New York, NY 10012
Copyright © 2020 by Sandra K. Athans
Published by Scholastic Inc. All rights reserved.
Printed in the U.S.A.
First printing, January 2020.

1 2 3 4 5 6 7 8 9 10   40   25 24 23 22 21 20

Contents

Introduction

As a writing specialist, I'm fortunate to work daily with student writers in grades K through 12. This hands-on experience lets me closely explore how students develop their writing skills and how these skills advance across the grade levels. A simple inference in second grade becomes a thesis statement in sixth grade. The identification of a character trait in third grade becomes the topic of in-depth literary analysis in tenth grade. Witnessing the evolution of student skill in writing as it develops to its highest form—thoughtful and effective authentic expression—is an exceptional opportunity!

Most teachers agree, however, that many students struggle with writing. While this isn't new, there is growing concern over a sharpening decline in student writing. Teachers' informal classroom observations suggest that students' already weakened skills are becoming more fragile year after year. The reasons behind this are plentiful: the influence of social media on academic writing; an instructional slow-down as districts take time to align expectations with newly revised or newly emerging standards; changing levels of parental involvement; inefficient skill transfer from traditional methods to technology-based methods of writing; and others. Adding to the challenge is the lack of time most teachers have in their over-burdened schedules to reverse the writing crisis.

Standardized test data further supports that writing has taken a hit in classrooms across the nation. For example, New York State data shows that a majority of students received less than half of the eligible points on the written portion of the English Language Arts (ELA) assessment. Similar statistics appear in other states.

Adding to this, many of the prompts in writing are designed to assess students' reading abilities. Why, then, aren't more grade-level readers able to effectively demonstrate their reading comprehension in writing? Something is amiss! Helping students demonstrate their skill, knowledge, and understanding on tasks that combine reading and writing proficiency is the goal of *Quick & Easy Strategies for Close Reading and Writing*.

A Next-Generation Approach to Advanced Literacies

The quick and easy strategies and lessons you're about to discover result from my practical classroom experiences. **They emphasize strategies useful for response writing, which is when students answer questions that are prompted by specific texts they must first read.** Other common terms used for this type of writing include constructed responses, on-demand writing, prompt-based writing, and even real-time writing. The strategies also help with other source-based writing, such as research papers or argumentative essays. For both, students draw upon their reading skills and their writing skills as they merge ideas gleaned from texts with their own original thinking.

I have come to believe that the merging of reading and writing represents a unique form of literacy that requires a unique skill set. We read and respond to texts differently when we

FIGURE 1

know we will be returning to them to retrieve ideas and information. Likewise, when we write from sources, our original ideas emerge and take shape based on the ways in which we choose to use the ideas of others. This merged reading-writing literacy is as important as the other "new literacies" that enrich our 21st-century curriculum. Figure 1 (right) lists a selection of 21st-century skills for students and teachers. Merged reading and writing skills are must-haves, too!

Many state standards newly recognize and address the changing nature of literacy. Today, there are calls for advanced literacies, which encompass mastery of diverse methods of communicating to diverse audiences. "This requires writing with precision, reading with understanding, and speaking in ways that communicate thinking clearly," as reflected in New York State's Next Generation Standards. Also emphasized in numerous state standards is the need to retain, preserve, and heighten the value of key literacy basics in reading and writing. New York State, for example, recognizes the critical nature of these must-haves, creating a separate category referred to as "Lifelong Practices." Similarities between these advanced literacies and the vast collage of 21st-century skills abound. Figure 2 (below) lists lifelong practices in reading and writing.

21st-Century Skills

For the 21st century, students must have ways of acquiring and knowing information from vast knowledge bases. The skills and knowledge need to be integrated and not separate.

Some 21st-century skills are:
1. critical thinking
2. problem solving
3. global awareness
4. collaboration

Teacher strategies for the 21st century should include:
1. problem- and project-based learning
2. authentic problem solving
3. engagement with students, colleagues, and the community
4. student-centered learning
5. technology integration

FIGURE 2

Lifelong Practices of Readers

Readers . . .
- think, write, speak, and listen to understand
- read often and widely from a range of global and diverse texts
- read for multiple purposes, including for learning and for pleasure
- self-select texts based on interest
- persevere through challenging, complex texts
- enrich personal language, background knowledge, and vocabulary through reading and communicating with others
- monitor comprehension and apply reading strategies flexibly
- make connections (to self, other texts, ideas, cultures, eras, etc.)

Lifelong Practices of Writers

Writers . . .
- think, read, speak, and listen to support writing
- write often and widely in a variety of formats, using print and digital resources and tools
- write for multiple purposes, including for learning and for pleasure
- persevere through challenging writing tasks
- enrich personal language, background knowledge, and vocabulary through writing and communicating with others
- experiment and play with language
- analyze mentor texts to enhance writing
- strengthen writing by planning, revising, editing, rewriting, or trying a new approach

Source: www.nysed.gov/common/nysed/files/introduction-to-the-nys-english-language-arts-standards.pdf

It's clear from teacher conversations as well as from test data that the time has come for change. In addition to restoring high-quality writing instruction, we must also make sure that students can reliably demonstrate the breadth and scope of their writing skill on classroom assignments as well as on standardized assessments, which includes the use of computer-based testing (CBT). Advancing traditional as well as electronic forms of our students' assessment writing is a shared nationwide goal. This initiative is especially timely as we enter a new phase of the standards evolution and, in turn, review our own instructional practices. The timing couldn't be more perfect!

In keeping with these ideas, the strategies and lessons in this book are not simply test-taking strategies to heighten students' proficiency scores on a test. While they will certainly help do that, the goal is broader. The featured strategies have far-reaching effects beyond the test; they encourage student growth toward writing authenticity and voice and away from formula. This gives the strategies their sticking power! In other words, they serve students well now and will also serve them well in the future as they make their way into the 21st century.

Buzz & Chatter

Computer-Based Testing (CBT)

Computer-based testing (CBT) is currently underway nationwide. While some states currently administer English language arts, math, and other standardized tests electronically, many others are in transition. Some states offer both CBT and pencil-and-paper testing; others have launched CBT pilots or field tests at select grade levels; still others are in the middle of planning their move to CBT. Meeting state goals to be up and running with computer testing is in progress!

No matter where your state falls along the implementation spectrum, you'll find the information in this book current and helpful. Despite changes to the way in which we test students, their proficiency with the language arts—including reading comprehension and analysis, writing to demonstrate and support understanding, writing from sources to generate original ideas, and writing with a command of style and mechanics—remain. Strengthening student skill at the crossroad where reading and writing merge is the critical objective of this work—the objective remains aligned with the content objectives of the language arts CBT.

Computer-based testing on such a large scale is also new for most school districts. It is also likely to change and improve over time, in keeping with the nature of the changing technology that supports it. As a result, helping students learn, practice, and master reading-writing literacy with scaffolded strategies as presented in this resource is paramount to teaching them ever-changing strategies that are dependent upon and therefore limited by the "latest" in computer-based tools. Such an approach could be misguided and shortsighted.

Still, meeting somewhere in the middle, so our students can comfortably, confidently, and capably demonstrate what they know on a computer as we transition into CBT, seems appropriate. As a result, suggestions for ways in which students can use common computer-based tools to support the strategies and scaffolds presented in this resource appear throughout.

Attitude Matters

Nothing helps build a can-do attitude faster than confidence, and nothing helps build confidence faster than know-how.

Teaching know-how to students in Grades 3 to 6 is what this book is all about. Here, the specific kind of know-how helps our students tackle tasks that require their use of both reading and writing skills. Response writing, in which students write short and extended answers to text-based questions, unite and merge these literacy skills.

We know this type of writing is a major challenge for our students for a lot of different reasons. One of the most common is that many feel that expressing their ideas in writing is just plain hard and demanding, not to mention time-consuming. No doubt these students would be mostly right. After all, writing takes much thought, and some form of a writing process—plan, draft, revise, edit—is a must! Both require energy and time.

For other students, the trouble begins earlier. Their struggles to read, understand, and interpret text drain their energy and stamina. For these students, the experience of demonstrating their reading and writing skills together in a single task is like running an endurance marathon that begins with a series of high hurdles. Clearly, their struggles compound an already difficult task.

While the challenges are many, there are ways we can help. Quick and easy ways to help students meet with greater success on tasks that merge these skills is the essence of this book.

A Pathway for Building Success: Close Reading, Structured Writing, and Critical Thinking

While most teachers have some degree of experience with close reading in their classroom, today it makes good sense to look closely at it. **Close reading is a method of reading carefully, deeply, and analytically to grasp a text as its author intended.** Maximizing the value of this reading approach is a must when helping students with response writing.

It is equally important to look closely at the type of response writing students have to do after they read. Structured writing provides students with a plan to address an array of prompted tasks. The structure helps direct and guide their writing. Determining what elements to include and how to organize these elements is one benefit of structured writing. Another benefit is that structured writing serves students as a temporary scaffold until their confidence and ability develops. Structured writing does not need to be permanent. Rather, it is best considered a flexible and temporary aid.

Buzz & Chatter

Temporary Scaffolds

It's important to keep in mind that many of the scaffolds used in this book are temporary. Such is the nature of scaffolds. Once students develop an understanding and then routinely practice, apply, and eventually master the way to solve a problem, they no longer need the scaffold. As an example, the Question-Attack strategies (page 47), which call for students to actively mark and code questions, are no longer needed once students master their ability to deeply understand what questions are asking. Rather than circle or underline key elements of a question to analyze it, a simple highlight—if that—may be all that is necessary.

Helping our students analyze fiction and nonfiction passages may seem like a tall order. Further guiding them in ways to use their analysis to formulate and express new, original ideas in writing may seem an even greater quest. However, beginning and developing this kind of critical thinking and critical composing is at the core of building lifelong, impassioned readers, writers, and collaborators. Starting here, now, with you as their guide, is a fine beginning.

As you are amidst the early stages of your students' analytical instruction, it may be helpful to keep in the mind the long-term intent and goal: **Literary analysis is examining the different elements of a piece of literature to help readers better appreciate and understand its work as a whole.** No doubt helping our students gain an understanding and appreciation of works of literature and informational texts is at the heart of all reading and writing activity. As such, strategies to help build critical thinking, analysis, and critical composing skills appear in all chapters within this book. Uniting our knowledge and savvy with close reading, structured writing, and critical thinking makes for the kind of powerful approach taken in this work. Yet, the unique strengths do not stop there.

How This Book Is Organized

While the strategies and lessons in this book are helpful for response writing and writing from sources, the emphasis is on the former. Still it is important to note that while some teachers might believe response writing is most often used for test-taking, this is only partially true. The use and application of nearly all of the strategies featured here are useful for real-world writing. The resounding message is that "teaching to the test" is often misguided criticism that does not take into account the fact that students are learning, practicing, and mastering strategies that are useful for good, solid reading and writing! While a rich, diverse, and flexibly balanced curriculum is best, perhaps it's time to revisit this long-standing criticism and consider creative ways to advance all writing—even that most associated with test-taking.

To accomplish this, the book is divided into four chapters. The strategy lessons are organized in a sequence that matches how a student would use them, beginning with close reading and then moving to the written response.

Chapter 1 focuses on quick and easy strategies for close reading. The lessons in this chapter highlight two distinct sets of strategies: Jump-Start strategies for prereading and Text-Marking strategies for annotating text. The Jump-Start strategies help students set expectations and launch their engagement and active participation in reading. The Text-Marking strategies help students monitor, track, and note their understanding as they move through the text.

Chapters 2 and 3 cover response writing, starting with short-response writing and followed by extended-response writing. While there are some similarities between the two, there are also enough differences or unique applications of the strategies to warrant covering them in separate chapters. Using the acronym RACE (Restate, Answer, Cite evidence, and Edit)—which represents an approach for writing a structured response—is one of the many powerful strategies covered in these chapters. Other strategies help students understand question prompts, gather critical evidence, and generate and express original ideas.

Chapter 4 moves students beyond structured writing. It addresses how to help students move away from a structured or formulaic approach to response writing. In addition to featuring fun and inviting strategies, these lessons encourage students to gauge their readiness and comfort level to explore and discover their unique voice and style of writing. A readiness checklist, compiled from independent surveys within each chapter, is included.

The **appendix** includes reproducible anchor texts and classroom-ready checklists, graphic organizers, and other skill-building handouts to support strategy instruction.

 Bonus Online Materials: Student-response exemplars are provided online. To access these extra resources, go to **www.scholastic.com/closereading andwriting** and enter your email address and access code **SC818834**.

The Quick & Easy Strategies and Lessons

To welcome the strategies comfortably into your classroom, I strongly recommend that you glance over the lessons to see the direction, intent, and materials available to you (e.g., anchor text passages, "master" student responses, and other classroom-ready resources). While some explanation is provided at the start of each chapter, the lessons and materials—like pictures— paint a thousand words. The visual nature of this resource is intended to support its "quick and easy" theme.

Each chapter begins with an overview of the reading or writing strategies. The lessons that follow come in a simplified format and introduce, build, and connect the strategies together. They are "good beginnings" yet will require follow-up classroom practice, which comes in the form of Close-Ups (described below) as well as other instructional pathways. The lessons are scripted in an easy-to-follow *italicized* font and come with discussion suggestions that guide you through key ideas and concepts. Below is a short description of each lesson's components.

Lesson Number and Title You may choose to present the lessons in order, double up on lessons, or selectively pick and choose the ones you would like to use, based on your specific needs. You may even combine elements from multiple lessons or do some other minor adaptations, as needed.

Quick Start A suggested prompt begins the lesson. You can write or project the prompt on a whiteboard, computer, or tablet screen; share it orally with students; or prepare it as a handout with other lesson materials.

Making Connections This provides a quick way to level student understanding at the start of a lesson. As students move from one grade level to the next or from one classroom to another, their understanding of terms, ideas, and concepts may differ. This time-saving component unifies and levels a shared understanding quickly.

Close-Ups While the lessons are intentionally brief in explaining the strategy to students, they are detailed in showing the strategies in action through Close-Ups. Here, master anchor texts and/or student-response exemplars (provided online) serve as models to scaffold understanding and help all students succeed. The Close-Ups achieve this in several ways:

1. by demonstrating all or part of a task
2. by showing how a strategy may be adapted or applied in a new way
3. by gradually increasing the difficulty level of a task

When used together, the Close-Ups in this system create a "comfort scaffolding" that helps students accept new challenges more readily. You can find reproducible versions of the anchor texts in the appendix (page 103) and download a printable PDF of student-response exemplars from the provided link (see page 9). You can display them on a whiteboard using a document camera, tablet, or other projectable or share-friendly device, or distribute photocopies to students.

Skill Builders These checklists, step-by-step guides, and other skill-building visuals, available in the appendix, reinforce or support students' close reading, structured writing, and/or critical thinking strategies. To share and use these visuals with students, you can:

1. project them on a whiteboard
2. display them on share-friendly technology
3. rewrite and post them on chart paper
4. distribute hard copies

These "skill builders" help students grasp concepts by providing critical information that may not have been mastered by everyone, breaking down a multistep process into smaller tasks, or reminding students of all of the components in a critical task. These visuals serve as models students can use as they develop a level of comfort and signs of success with independent application.

Quick Close A suggested highlight to wrap up the lesson.

Independent Readiness Survey Each lesson concludes with a quick survey to help students assess their own level of independent readiness. While this encourages students to gauge their level of understanding, you will also find the survey results useful to differentiate further instruction, as needed. Chapter 4 includes surveys on all of the close-reading, writing, and thinking strategies and practices that appear throughout this book. It is a worthwhile exercise to have students take the survey after they have benefited from repeated practice and are considering how to make the strategies their own.

Teaching Notes These helpful suggestions provide some insight into the difficulty level of each strategy and how to differentiate and/or scaffold it for all students, the many ways in which the strategy can be useful beyond test-taking, and tips on how to integrate practice within the routine of classroom activity.

Flexible Root Lessons

The lessons included in this book are "root lessons" because they are the essentials and contain critical, grounding concepts. You can adapt them as you choose; for example, by adding to and/or refining the instruction as you deem appropriate. You can also change the order of the lessons, as well as tailor them in a number of other ways to suit your needs. (See "Lesson Presentation" online for alternative ways to present the lessons in this book.)

It is also important to note that the reading strategies and the structured writing strategies repeat even when the nature of the task may be different. For example, close-reading strategies are similar for literature and informational texts, with some modifications. Likewise, the structured approach for writing a response about character traits may mimic the structure of a response about theme. This is done intentionally. Helping students recognize the flexible and adaptive nature of their reading and writing skills encourages them to explore their multifunctional use when applying them independently.

Moving Forward ... Beyond the Test and Beyond the Structure

While there is merit in teaching text-based writing using a highly-structured approach, the greater goal is to enable students to communicate their original ideas skillfully and engagingly. There is no reason why response writing must be confined to a test-taking formula that plods along unconvincingly in the mind of the writer and the ear of the reader. Unintentional yet shortsighted thinking has hampered our advances with this kind of writing . . . until now! Moving students beyond the scaffolds toward independent success with high-level, authentic expression in their text-based writing is the direction *Quick & Easy Strategies for Close Reading and Writing* takes.

The strategies and approaches in this book encourage good thinking and good writing overall—they represent lifelong practices that serve students well, now and in the future. They also teach students how to apply skills most often associated with test-taking to authentic, engaging writing projects and demonstrate how to extend the benefits of this type of writing. These pragmatic lessons are useful not only for any reading-writing, standards-based classroom instruction, they also forge a new direction for reshaping traditional test-preparation instruction.

It is my hope that you will apply and adapt the strategies suggested here to suit your purpose. "Use this as you wish" is the sentiment I extend to the worldwide network of teaching professionals who read my books. It is my way to invite you into the pages, a way to welcome your collaboration, and a way to honor your professionalism! It is also my way to thank you for joining me in this new literacy adventure.

Preparing for the Journey

To prepare students for their text-based writing journey, we open with an introductory lesson that offers a preview of what lies ahead.

This book is unique in that it develops Super Readers-Writers-Thinkers! It does this by sharing simple strategies that help all elementary-level students—including struggling readers and writers—gain skill and confidence with these demanding tasks by uniting very powerful close-reading techniques with highly effective writing scaffolds. In addition, the strategies in this book help students develop critical thinking and critical composing routines to plan, launch, and construct their ideas, making these kinds of tasks more manageable.

The following introductory lesson articulates and shares this important goal: to help students build their skills—and adopt a positive attitude—with tasks that call for reading and writing together.

LESSON 1 — Quick & Easy Ways to Become a Super Reader-Writer-Thinker!

Quick Start: When have you used reading and writing together?

Making Connections

Tell students: *Sometimes we use reading and writing together at home. Other times we use them together at school. Can you give some examples of when we use reading and writing together at home?* (Sample responses: Reading and responding to notes/emails/messages from parents; filling out forms to join a sports team, get a library card, or open a bank account) *What about in school?* (Reading a story/article/book and answering questions; reading about turtles and writing a research report about them; reading teacher and classmate notes/blogs/posts/journals and answering questions/adding a response)

Invite students to imagine for a moment: *If you could have any reading-writing superpower to help with these tasks or others, what would it be?* (Sample responses: High-speed reading and writing; magic glasses and magic pencil and an eraser cape; telepathy to understand everything in a story, article, or book through touch; or answer questions or share ideas through brainwave transfer)

Tell students: *Even if we can only imagine some of these superpowers, there are ways we can become Super Readers and Super Writers and Super Thinkers! Let's take a look at some "Close-Ups" to see how.*

Close-Up #1: Be a Super Reader

Display the "Be a Super Reader" mini-poster (page 104) on the whiteboard. Ask students: *Did you know there are some quick and easy tricks or strategies to help you read? Do you see some you know? Are there some you don't know? We are going to learn and practice them all.*

Close-Up #2: Be a Super Writer

Next, display the "Be a Super Writer" mini-poster (page 105). Ask students: *Did you know that there are some quick and easy tricks or strategies to help you write? Do you see some you know? Are there some you don't know? We are going to learn and practice them all.*

(See Appendix, pages 104 and 105.)

Close-Up #3: Be a Super Thinker

Finally, display the "Be a Super Thinker" mini-poster (page 106). Ask students: *Did you know that there are some quick and easy tricks or strategies to help you think? Do you see some you know? Are there some you don't know? We are going to learn and practice them all.*

Quick Close

Say to students: *Lucky for you, sign-ups are today! If you're interested in becoming a Super Reader-Writer-Thinker and learning about these quick and easy tricks or strategies, put on your magic glasses, grab your magic pencil (or stylus), and "air sign" your name.*

Independent Readiness Survey

Gauge students' level of spirit and confidence at becoming Super Reader-Writer-Thinkers. Read the numbered statements below and have students respond in one of three ways:

(See Appendix, page 106.)

- Thumbs up if they agree
- Thumbs down if they disagree
- Thumbs midway if they half agree

1. I'm excited to be a Super Reader-Writer-Thinker!
2. Learning quick and easy ways to be a Super Reader — I can do that!
3. Learning quick and easy ways to be a Super Writer — I can do that!
4. Learning quick and easy ways to stay super alert and thinking — I can do that!

Teaching Notes

- Explain to the class that some students find reading-writing tasks challenging. Reassure students that the "Quick & Easy" (Q & E) strategies they will learn in upcoming lessons will build their skills and prepare them well. As a result, the tasks won't seem so challenging.

- Reinforce your upbeat approach and long-term intention to foster positive student attitude throughout the Q & E lessons. Praise student success, welcome original thinking, and model your love of reading-writing literacy.

- Support struggling learners by monitoring them during the Q & E lessons and by helping them during other practice times. Gauge their level of participation and take note of their self-assessment at the end of the lesson. (Ways to integrate additional classroom practice for all of the strategies are provided in the Teaching Notes section of every lesson.)

- Link the Q & E lessons with other initiatives your school district may be undertaking. Character education, academic excellence, and other schoolwide themes are well-suited to the positive, can-do attitude you're encouraging for reading-writing literacy development.

CHAPTER 1

Quick & Easy Strategies for Close Reading

Do your students read everything the same way? There are as many different ways to read as there are reasons to read. Experienced readers know this. They may quickly skim articles in newspapers, savor the latest release of a favorite author, wade slowly through step-by-step assembly directions, or scan scrolling text across an electronic device. Adjusting their pace, attentiveness, and methods of advancing through a text come automatically to experienced readers. This is not true of inexperienced readers, including many of our students. They have yet to discover alternatives to a "one-way" approach to reading. (See Figure 3: "Ways to Read," page 17.)

Close reading opens the door to such discovery. In *Close Reading for the Whole Class*, a teacher resource book I co-authored, we provide this robust, student-friendly definition of the approach: "Close reading is a method of reading carefully, deeply, and analytically to grasp a text as its author intended." This technique is not intended for what many would consider "light" reading. Rather, an effective way to close-read a text would be to read it slowly and intentionally. Another way would be to pause and reflect. Still another way would be to reread—at least once, if not possibly twice—to clarify and deepen understanding. These simple "adjustments" are basic reading strategies. Experienced readers may readily call them into action. Inexperienced readers may not. We will touch upon these simple strategies in the lessons within this chapter, but the emphasis is reserved for much more powerful tools. While most teachers model the simple adjustment strategies regularly, new ways to use them with merged reading-writing tasks can deepen our ever-growing repertoire of expertise.

We can foster students' deep reading by engaging them with the text from start to finish. Strategies to help rally their interest and sustain their interaction become part of our close-reading routine. Close reading is also well paired with writing prompts and tasks because students must often return to the text to respond. Knowing a text well—through close reading—helps with this process.

Powerful Close-Reading Strategies

In addition to basic strategies in which readers adjust pace, attentiveness, and movement through the text, we use other strategies in close reading. These include the Jump-Start strategy and Text-Marking strategies.

The Jump-Start Strategy—Reading With Purpose

The objective of the Jump-Start strategy is to help students read with purpose. The strategy empowers students to independently activate and apply their growing literary knowledge and skills to set goals in advance of their reading. The Jump-Start strategy also helps students monitor their reading as they shape, reshape, and build their understanding.

Students will quickly scan the passage they are about to read and apply their background literary knowledge to predict whether a passage is fact (informational or nonfiction) or fiction (narrative story or literature). Based on their prediction, they then create a mental checklist of things they will seek out as they begin to read. In essence, students use their growing literary knowledge to launch a very flexible set of expectations for their reading.

Two lessons are included in the Jump-Start strategy. The first introduces students to predicting and prepares them to set their reading expectations. The second shows them how to monitor and adjust their expectations as they read.

Text-Marking Strategies—Real-Time Annotating

Text-Marking strategies also help students read in a close-reading way. These strategies enable students to track their reading and note and shape their deep thinking (analysis) of a text in real-time, as they read. In addition, the codes and symbols they use to mark the text will prove especially helpful when they return to their reading passage to respond to prompted tasks—either multiple-choice questions or writing tasks. Often in such cases, students must seek evidence in the text to demonstrate their understanding or to support their original thinking. Their text-markings make the process of returning to the text swift and targeted.

Students will read and note their thinking directly on the text or on sticky notes. They will learn four basic types of text-marking, enabling them to annotate texts flexibly.

1. underlining
2. coding
3. writing gist statements
4. labeling text with # (hashtags)

We will teach these strategies over three lessons. The first lesson introduces the basics of underlining and coding. The second offers suggestions for other helpful codes for marking text. The third presents the more powerful techniques of writing gist statements and labeling text using # (hashtags). All of the lessons address the unique differences between text-marking informational text and nonfiction as compared to text-marking works of literature and fiction.

Computer-Based Testing and Close Reading/Text-Marking

The kinds of tools and capabilities students will have to complete their computer-based test depends upon the platform the test administers choose. For the most part, students will have access to highlighting, underlining, and note-taking tools, as well as inserting tools and a cut-and-paste function, among others (including tools designed to help with specialized test accommodations, such as those assigned to a student's Individualized Education Plan).

During close reading and text-marking, students can highlight and/or underline keywords and ideas in their text. They may also use the insert function to record hashtags (#). Advancing students' text-marking skills so they internalize the early engagement tactics—such as emoticon happy faces, exclamation marks, and other basic strategies shared in this chapter—will best serve our students over time. Once they have mastered and internalized these skills, they can begin to eliminate some text-marking strategies. After all, we do not want to congest a passage with so many marks that it becomes impossible to navigate with speed and intent.

The routine practice and mastery of close reading and text-marking a passage to deepen comprehension, ignite swift recall, and target a search for evidence hot spots are easily accomplished using the tools available through most CBT platforms.

Recapping the Benefits of Close-Reading Strategies

All of these powerful sets of close-reading strategies—from basic ways to adjust reading pace, attentiveness, and movement through text, to the more powerful Jump-Start and Text-Marking strategies—help students deepen their understanding and develop analytical skills. Experienced close readers wield them masterfully, and inexperienced close readers will significantly increase their level of success as Super Reader-Writer-Thinkers by learning and applying them. Helping young readers learn and apply basic and analytical strategies is the emphasis of the lessons in this chapter. (Chapters 2 and 3 discuss ways in which these strategies also help students prepare for writing tasks.)

In launching students' discovery of these strategies, we not only celebrate their active role in reading but we also help ignite their appreciation of good, solid writing. Our coordinated efforts to guide them on this journey—through direct instruction, practice, patience, and encouragement—are well worth it!

FIGURE 3

Ways to Read

Some Ways to Read and Move Through Text	What It Looks Like	Types of Reading Material	Reader's Objective
Skim	Quickly moving across text	Newspapers	To seek main ideas or facts; some surface-level understanding is OK
Savor	Slow, lingering pauses; halting to dwell on words, ideas, and events	New book from a favorite author	To enjoy/take in the text fully
Wade	Slow, pausing, some read aloud to clarify; rereading and backtracking	Step-by-step assembly directions or recipes	To grasp sequenced or complex ideas
Lumber	Halting, pausing, stopping, reflecting; chunking text	Content-rich or specialized information	To make sense of dense text that may include jargon, unfamiliar facts, complex ideas
Scan	Quickly moving across text; some pausing if/when needed information is detected	Emails, text messages, tweets, and other electronic texts	To take in short electronic messages or to quickly search an entire electronic text for needed information
Jockey (1)	Moving from text to visual—or visual to text; varied pace, with pauses and repeats; lingering	Graphic novels, comics, illustrated texts; picture books; texts with visuals	To blend words and visuals to grasp meaning
Jockey (2)	Moving from text to other text— in multiple directions	Screen text (electronic device) with embedded links	To gather vast breadth and scope; to follow suggested linked ideas
March (rhythm)	Adjusting pacing and pausing based on the rhythm of a text	Poetry, song lyrics, other metered texts	To enjoy poetry, song lyrics

LESSON 2

Close Reading and Close-Reading Strategies

Guide students to discover what it means to close-read and how reading in a "close-reading way" can help them uncover more in a passage.

Quick Start: What is close reading? When would we use it?

Making Connections

Tell students: *Close reading is careful reading. It is a method of reading with purpose. That purpose is to learn information, discover ideas, and build skills. You'll also come to recognize and value good writing. Close reading also lets us notice or detect new things we might not have noticed before. Let's take a close look!*

Close-Up #1: Palindromes

Write these sentences on the board:

> **1.** Now I won!
> **2.** Was it a hat I saw?

Tell students: *Look closely at these sentences. Can you figure out the puzzle in sentence #1 and "win" too?* (The sentence reads the same backward and forward.) *Even though we have to read beyond the capital letters and spacing, we can detect this pattern. Do you see a similar pattern in sentence #2? While these texts are puzzles, all authors arrange words, sentences, paragraphs, and chapters in ways that matter. Reading closely helps us see this.*

Close-Up #2: Dollar Bill

Display a dollar bill on the board. Tell students: *Look closely at the dollar bill. What are some things you've never seen before?* (Sample responses: Clusters of leaves, different shapes encircling the number 1, an eagle holding arrows and a branch) *We're all familiar with a dollar bill, but we may have detected new things. Although these are objects, not text, the example shows us that "reading" closely helps us see new things.*

Close-Up #3: The Star-Spangled Banner

On the board, write the following questions:

> **1.** What is "The Star-Spangled Banner"?
> **2.** What does the word *perilous* mean?

Next, display the lyrics to "The Star-Spangled Banner" (page 107) on the board. Say to students: *Look closely. Follow along as I read aloud from the original "Star-Spangled Banner." Try to detect clues to help with the two questions listed on the board.*

(See Appendix, page 107.)

APPENDIX Lesson 2

The Star-Spangled Banner
by Francis Scott Key

O say can you see, by the dawn's early light,

What so proudly we hail'd at the twilight's last gleaming,

Whose broad stripes and bright stars through the perilous fight

O'er the ramparts we watch'd were so gallantly streaming?

And the rocket's red glare, the bombs bursting in air,

Gave proof through the night that our flag was still there,

O say does that star-spangled banner yet wave

O'er the land of the free and the home of the brave?

Ask: *What are some clues that help us answer question 1?* (Sample responses: There are broad stripes and bright stars, so it's probably a flag; line 6 says it is a flag; it streams and waves, which are movements of a flag.) *What are some clues that help us answer question 2?* (It is used to describe a "fight," so it may mean something bad; there were glaring rockets and bombs bursting, so it was an all-out fight.)

Tell students: *These examples show that reading closely helps us learn new information and new vocabulary words. Now, look closely as I read it again. I'm going to read the text exactly as the author arranged and punctuated it. Do you notice something new?* (Sample response: There are two question marks in the passage, so the author is asking if the flag was still there. The author wanted us to read those lines as questions.)

It seems we saw and learned something new. In order to detect these new "finds" we had to read in a different kind of way. We had to adjust our reading to read in a close-reading way. Let's review all of the strategies we used. Display the "Take Action Close-Reading Strategies Checklist" (page 108) on the board and discuss with the class.

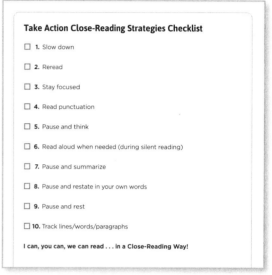

(See Appendix, page 108.)

Quick Close

Say to students: *From our Close-Ups, we've learned that close reading is a special way of reading. Sometimes we change the way we read so we can learn and discover new things.*

Independent Readiness Survey

Gauge students' comfort level with close reading and the new strategies they have learned. Read the numbered statements below and have students respond in one of three ways:

- Thumbs up if they agree
- Thumbs down if they disagree and want more guided practice with a teacher
- Thumbs midway if they almost agree but would like to work with a partner

1. I know close reading is a special way to read carefully.
2. I can independently make changes to the way I read by slowing down, rereading, and by using other strategies we learned today.
3. I am prepared to learn and practice all of the close-reading strategies so I can tell which ones will help me the most.

Teaching Notes

- Use short passages (such as articles) or an excerpt from a book-length work to easily integrate close reading into your planned instruction. Longer works may require too much instructional time. Short sessions of routine practice are best as students try out the strategies.

- To help students overcome "racing" through a text, you may want to introduce a reading routine for students to follow. For example, students might use a strategy bookmark or sticky note to try out and share several specific strategies. Use the Take Action Close-Reading Strategies Checklist as a bookmark or single out a strategy, such as "Slow down," and have students put a sticky note where they found this strategy helpful in a text.

- Many of the strategies used with close reading are also effective for general reading instruction. You may wish to use close reading while working with differentiated guided-reading groups as well as with whole-class grade-level instruction. Alter your scaffolds to support students as needed.

- Monitor student use of the close-reading strategies to ensure there is a comfortable mix of analysis (rereading, pausing, and so on) and reading fluency. The process shouldn't overburden students.

- Close reading is one method of reading and should be considered one component of a larger reading program. Combine close reading with other methods of reading instruction as well as with read-aloud time, independent reading, content-area reading, and more.

Basic Jump-Start Strategy: Prereading for Fact or Fiction

Introduce students to prereading and how to apply their growing knowledge of literary basics to help them determine whether a text passage is fact or fiction.

Quick Start: What is prereading? What does it mean to preread for fact or fiction?

Making Connections

Tell students: *Prereading is like playing* I Spy, *only it's more like "advanced"* I Spy *because you're going beyond what you see by thinking about the importance of what you see. For example:* I spy _____, so I think _____. *This stretches our thinking.*

Prereading for fact or fiction means turning on your engines (thinking and activating knowledge) and seeking out clues that tell you whether your passage contains fact (is an article or informational text) or fiction (is a story or piece of literature). This happens even before you begin to read. Let's try it!

Close-Up #1: Picnic Tricks

Display "Picnic Tricks" (page 109) on the board. Tell students: *Look closely at this text passage. What do you spy on the page? What do you think—is it fact or fiction?*

Students will likely identify this piece as a story/fiction/literature based on the illustration. Point out that there are brief paragraphs and quotation marks, suggesting that an exchange of dialogue is taking place. Some students may say that the title suggests a playfulness that make it seem like fiction. Code this passage *S* for story (or *L* for literature).

(See Appendix, page 109.)

Think & Discuss: Advanced I Spy for Fiction/Literature

What's on the page?

- I spy *pictures*, so I think *this is a story*.

- I spy *many short paragraphs of dialogue (use of quotation marks)*, so I think *this is a story*.

- I spy _____ in the title, so I think this is a story about _____.

- Other ideas: _____

(See Appendix, page 115.)

Close-Up #2: When Looks Matter

Next, display "When Looks Matter" (page 110) on the board. Say: *Now, look closely at this other text passage. What do you spy on the page? What do you think—is it fact or fiction?*

Students will likely identify this piece as an informational text based on multiple features:

- **photographs:** three photos suggest real life
- **captions:** often used in nonfiction
- **subheadings:** looks like an article
- **boldface words:** vocabulary words are highlighted, which is common in nonfiction

Point out that many of the features look like those we see in other nonfiction or informational articles we read. Code this passage *A* for article (or *I* for informational text).

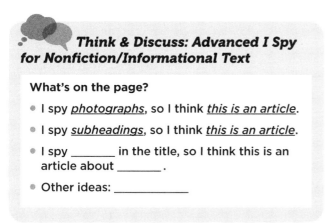

(See Appendix, page 110.)

Think & Discuss: Advanced I Spy for Nonfiction/Informational Text

What's on the page?

- I spy *photographs*, so I think *this is an article*.

- I spy *subheadings*, so I think *this is an article*.

- I spy _____ in the title, so I think this is an article about _____ .

- Other ideas: _____

(See Appendix, page 115.)

Say to students: *That was easy! Let's review what we know about stories and articles.* Display the "What I Know About..." chart (page 115) on the board and discuss.

Say: *These things "I know" now become "what I must uncover!"* Explain to students that as they read, they should be on the lookout to uncover those things that are likely to be in their text passage. In a fictional story, they should look for:

Think & Discuss: What I Know About...	
Most Stories	**Most Articles**
I know . . .	I know . . .
• in the beginning, a character has a problem.	• an author wants to inform us about a topic through text and possibly visuals.
• in the middle, the character tries to solve it through events.	• the author shares key ideas about the topic in paragraphs.
• in the end, there is a solution.	• each paragraph has details.
• the character learns something new.	• there are many kinds of details and many ways to tell about them.
• the reader learns a life lesson.	• the author makes an overall point (main idea) about the topic.
	• the reader learns information.

(See Appendix, page 115.)

- characters
- problem
- events
- solution
- theme (what the character learns)

In an informational text, they should look for:

- the topic
- key ideas in each paragraph
- how the details are told
- the author's point (main idea) about the topic

Tell students: *Remember, it's okay to change your mind about what genre a text might be and adjust your thinking.*

Note: Students are not going to read the passages to check their responses during this lesson. They will use the same passages for the lessons on text-marking, during which they will interact with the text more.

 For more practice, use additional text passages in the Appendix, pages 111–114.

Quick Close

Ask students: *Why do you suppose this is called the Jump-Start strategy?* (Sample response: We jump in and use clues to get us ready to read.) *We have ideas about our reading before we start, so we've jumped right in to making sense of the passage.*

Independent Readiness Survey

Gauge students' comfort level with using the basic Jump-Start strategies. Read the numbered statements below and have students respond in one of three ways:

- Thumbs up if they agree
- Thumbs down if they disagree and want more guided practice with a teacher
- Thumbs midway if they almost agree but would like to work with a partner

1. I can scan, think, and predict whether a passage is fictional or informational.
2. I can use what I already know about fictional and informational texts to help me set goals before I read.
3. I am prepared to use what I already know about fiction and informational texts to help guide me while I read.

Teaching Notes

- Provide students with a variety of reading passages so they can practice identifying fact or fiction effectively.

- Keep an eye out for students who may rely heavily on visuals instead of the structure of the text passage. Encourage them to use both clues as a check system.

- Students enjoy practicing with a variety of different grade-level passages. As they will not be reading the passage, this gives them the opportunity to gain confidence and have fun engaging in the Jump-Start strategy.

- Remind students that they need to remain flexible as they read. They may change their minds about what genre a text passage might be. Likewise, some stories may not follow the structure exactly. We are always shaping and reshaping our thinking and our ideas based on available information.

- Some students may get confused when trying to apply the Jump-Start strategy when there are mixed clues. Remind them that the process of thinking through their ideas and setting flexible expectations is more important than being right at the start, when they haven't read the passage.

LESSON 4 Extreme Jump-Start Strategy: Monitoring and Adjusting for Meaning

Show students how to divide a text passage into smaller, more manageable sections to help them monitor and adjust their expectations as they read.

Quick Start: What could add an element of "extreme" to our Jump-Start strategy? How can we "own" the strategy?

Making Connections

Tell students: *The word* extreme *suggests "kicking things up" or improving things. Now, we're going to kick up how we use our Jump-Start strategy while we read by staying tuned in and turned on! Let's quickly review.*

For stories (literature/fiction), students should plan to look for:
- characters
- problem
- events
- solution
- theme (what the character learns)

For articles (informational texts/nonfiction), they should plan to look for:
- the topic
- key ideas in each paragraph
- how the details were told
- the author's point (main idea) about the topic

Tell students: *Sometimes we're right about our prediction as to whether a passage is fictional or informational, and we can stick to our plan. But sometimes we're wrong. Then we have to change our plan of attack. Having confidence in our ability to use the Jump-Start strategy in this way helps us own it. Let's see this in action!*

Close-Up #1: Picnic Tricks

Display "Picnic Tricks" (page 109) on the board or hand out copies. Say to students: *Let's revisit "Picnic Tricks," which we coded S for story (or L for literature). We agreed that this looks mostly like a story. It has an illustration and brief paragraphs with quotation marks, suggesting dialogue. So now we're going to look for characters, a problem, events, a solution, and a theme (what the character learns). Let's read this together and discuss our findings in sections.*

Lesson 4 Close-Up #1

Picnic Tricks
by Jack Sprat

① "We're going to have the best picnic ever!" Tina called. She added grapes to a bright yellow lunch bag.

"Aw, Tina. Picnics are no fun," said Scooter. He leaned against the screen door. "Ants always sneak onto my sandwich. Sometimes I eat them by mistake!" He scowled. "They taste yucky."

② Tina stepped out to the porch, pulling the strap of the lunch bag over her shoulder. The door banged closed behind her.

"Doesn't have to be that way, Scooter," she said. She helped him off the porch and led the way to the backyard. "Always look for ants before taking a bite. If you see any, use the Flick Trick, like this." She ran her pointer finger quickly across the bottom of her thumb, pretending to flick an ant off her arm. "That's my trick for getting rid of pests on a picnic."

"Thanks, Tina," he said, stopping to test his flicking skills. He thought it was a good trick.

③ "I'd like to picnic near the ferns," Tina said, pointing to the part of her yard that butted up to Mrs. Major's house.

Scooter stopped in his tracks. "Aw, Tina. Not there! Zippy lives in the house by the ferns! When I play in my sandbox, he runs over and jumps on me. He licks my face all over." He cringed.

"Doesn't have to be that way, Scooter," Tina said, waving for him to catch up. "If Zippy visits our picnic, do the Scratch Trick." Tina hooked her thumbs together, spread her fingers and curled them slightly. "Bend down and give Zippy a good scratch behind his ears." She wiggled her fingers as if scratching. "That's my trick for keeping a jumpy puppy down on a picnic."

"Thanks, Tina," Scooter said, twisting his fingers into shape. He thought it was a good trick.

④ When they reached the fern bed, Tina found a perfect clearing. No sooner had she set the lunch bag down when — "Yap! Yap! Yap-pity, Yap!" — a frisky puppy sped toward them.

"Aw, Tina . . . It's ZIPPY!"

In a flash, Scooter had his doggy scratcher in place like a shield, but the frisky puppy lurched toward the lunch bag instead. He grabbed the strap and ran off.

"Stop, Zippy!" cried Tina, trailing after the thief. Sandwiches, grapes, and other treats flew from the lunch bag, which had come open in the commotion.

Scooter watched as Zippy led Tina on a high-speed chase until finally, the tired pooch dropped the emptied lunch bag and jogged home.

"Aw, Scooter," Tina said. "The puppy has made a mess of our lunch!" She scooped up some squished grapes and dropped them into the soiled lunch bag. "Our best picnic ever is in shambles."

Scooter wasn't used to seeing his friend without a fix-it trick . . . but perhaps it was now his turn.

"Aw, Tina, it doesn't have to be that way!" As Tina hunted through the ferns to clean up, Scooter ran back to his house and returned in no time. He was carrying a brown paper bag.

⑤ "One PBJ for you, and one PBJ for me." He handed Tina a sandwich. "Do-Overs!" he said. "That's my trick for fixing picnics." He flicked off an ant that had snuck onto his sandwich and smiled at Tina.

"Do-Overs!" she cheered. "That's the best trick ever!"

They each took a big bite of sandwich.

Draw lines, as shown at left, to divide the story into sections.

Q: In section 1, what do we find?
A: The characters and the problem. The characters are Tina and Scooter. The problem unfolds when we learn that Scooter doesn't like picnics. He doesn't share Tina's zest for them because ants get in his food.

Q: In section 2, what do we find?
A: The events begin. A key event takes place—Tina shows Scooter the Flick Trick.

Q: In section 3, what do we find?
A: The problem builds, and another key event takes place. Scooter doesn't like it when Zippy licks his face, and now the setting of the picnic—near Zippy's home—adds to Scooter's dislikes. Another key event is that Tina teaches Scooter the Scratch Trick.

Q: In section 4, what do we find?
A: An added problem/event peaks. The problem reaches a head when Zippy steals the lunch bag and ruins the food. This key event also ruins Tina's joyful attitude about the picnic.

Q: In section 5, what do we find?
A: The solution unfolds and the characters learn a lesson. Scooter devises the Do-Over Trick and saves the picnic. He not only learns creative ways to solve his problems, he also learns that he can be a problem solver. The theme is that we can solve problems creatively.

Say to students: *Using our Jump-Start strategy, we were on the lookout for characters, problems, events, solutions, and theme, or lesson learned—and we found them! We used our literary skills—what we know about stories—to help us.*

Close-Up #2: When Looks Matter

Next, display "When Looks Matter" (page 110) on the board or hand out copies. Say to students: *Let's revisit "When Looks Matter," which we coded as A for article (or I for informational). We agreed that this looks mostly like a nonfiction article. So now we'll look for the topic, key ideas in each paragraph, how the details are told, and the author's point (main idea) about the topic. Let's read this together and discuss our findings in sections.*

Draw lines, as shown at right, to divide the article into sections.

Q: In section 1, what do we find?
A: The topic, how details are told, and the author's point. While clues about the topic show up in the title and photographs—some animals look odd—we can also add that many are endangered. Scientist Lucy Cooke and the author's take on the topic is that we might want to help these animals.

Q: In section 2, what do we find?
A: The topic, how details are told, and the author's point. The topic builds. We learn ugly animals don't get as much help as cute ones. The author writes about differences in how we treat cute and ugly animals. The author tells us it's "bad news" because an ecosystem can be harmed if a species dies out.

Q: In section 3, what do we find?
A: The topic, how details are told, and the author's point. The topic grows. We learn animals may be ugly for protection. Cooke hopes we will want to save them. In this article, the author informs us that odd-looking animals are just as important as the cute ones and many may need our help to survive.

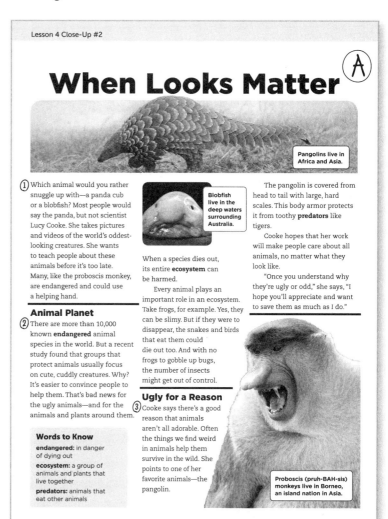

Lesson 4 Close-Up #2

When Looks Matter Ⓐ

Pangolins live in Africa and Asia.

① Which animal would you rather snuggle up with—a panda cub or a blobfish? Most people would say the panda, but not scientist Lucy Cooke. She takes pictures and videos of the world's oddest-looking creatures. She wants to teach people about these animals before it's too late. Many, like the proboscis monkey, are endangered and could use a helping hand.

Animal Planet
② There are more than 10,000 known **endangered** animal species in the world. But a recent study found that groups that protect animals usually focus on cute, cuddly creatures. Why? It's easier to convince people to help them. That's bad news for the ugly animals—and for the animals and plants around them.

Words to Know
endangered: in danger of dying out
ecosystem: a group of animals and plants that live together
predators: animals that eat other animals

Blobfish live in the deep waters surrounding Australia.

When a species dies out, its entire **ecosystem** can be harmed.
Every animal plays an important role in an ecosystem. Take frogs, for example. Yes, they can be slimy. But if they were to disappear, the snakes and birds that eat them could die out too. And with no frogs to gobble up bugs, the number of insects might get out of control.

Ugly for a Reason
③ Cooke says there's a good reason that animals aren't all adorable. Often the things we find weird in animals help them survive in the wild. She points to one of her favorite animals—the pangolin.

The pangolin is covered from head to tail with large, hard scales. This body armor protects it from toothy **predators** like tigers.
Cooke hopes that her work will make people care about all animals, no matter what they look like.
"Once you understand why they're ugly or odd," she says, "I hope you'll appreciate and want to save them as much as I do."

Proboscis (pruh-BAH-sis) monkeys live in Borneo, an island nation in Asia.

Say to students: *Using the Jump-Start strategy, we were on the lookout for topics, how the details were told, and the author's point (main idea) about the topic—and we found them! We used what we know about articles/informational texts to help us. Nicely done!*

 For more practice, use additional text pages in the Appendix, pages 111–114.)

Quick Close

Say to students: *How have we built our extreme skills with the Jump-Start strategy? In "Picnic Tricks" and "When Looks Matter," we used our Jump-Start strategy to help us look for things in the passage as we read. Reading carefully, we confirmed our predictions that "Picnic Tricks" is a story and "When Looks Matter" is an article. We also found the elements we were looking for.*

Independent Readiness Survey

Gauge students' comfort level with using the Extreme Jump-Start strategy. Read the numbered statements below and have students respond in one of three ways:

- Thumbs up if they agree
- Thumbs down if they disagree and want more guided practice with a teacher
- Thumbs midway if they almost agree but would like to work with a partner

1. As I begin reading, I can independently use the Jump-Start strategy and flexibly change my plan for reading.
2. As I begin reading, I can independently use the Jump-Start strategy and adapt my plan for reading.
3. I have confidence in my ability to use the Extreme Jump-Start strategy skills!

Teaching Notes

- The Extreme Jump-Start strategy is easy to integrate into your planned instruction. It's likely you'll soon start noticing passages that look quirky or unusual or that present information in an unusual way. Save and use them for this lesson.

- Students may get confused when trying to apply the Jump-Start strategy to realistic fiction and narrative nonfiction. ("Deep in the Ocean" [page 111] and "Ask Joan the Bone Hunter" [page 112] are good examples of these.) Including samples of these genres will help build and strengthen student skill.

- Gauge how to best use scaffolds. Determine how to maximize your use of modeling, guiding instruction, and independent practice as you use tricky passages. Be prepared to change your strategy based on student experience and comfort level.

- Some students may need further practice to flexibly adapt the Jump-Start strategy. Continued practice will provide them with the confidence to monitor their thinking and value their judgments. Expand their experiences with applying the strategy to complex passages to strengthen their literary understandings.

- Students may need to develop their stamina as they work through more challenging or lengthier passages. To help students build stamina, you may want to alternate between whole-class reading (with guided think-alouds) and independent reading. This may be easier than trying to locate passages that have "ideal" lengths.

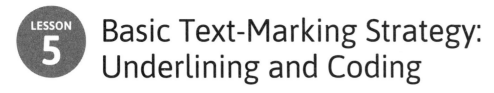

LESSON 5

Basic Text-Marking Strategy: Underlining and Coding

Help students build understanding by using underlines and codes to detect and note key elements in the text.

Quick Start: Get ready to read with a pencil! What exactly does that mean?

Making Connections

Say to students: *Reading with a pencil (point down) helps us a lot. We can:*

- *"track," or follow, the text so we don't miss anything.*
- *make notes as we read to show our thinking.*
- *use this strategy with other close-reading strategies, such as the Jump-Start strategy.*

Explain that reading with a pencil is an effective way to note our thoughts and interact with the text as we read.

Close-Up #1: Picnic Tricks

Tell students: *Let's get ready to read with our pencils! We're going to revisit "Picnic Tricks," which we coded S in our previous lesson, based on our Jump-Start prediction that it is a story. Remember, we want to look out for story elements: characters, problem, events, solution, and theme (what the character learns). Let's see how we can use text-marking to support our search.*

Display "Picnic Tricks" (page 109) on the board and hand out copies. Go over the displayed text together and have students follow along on their hard copy as you think aloud and text-mark the passage.

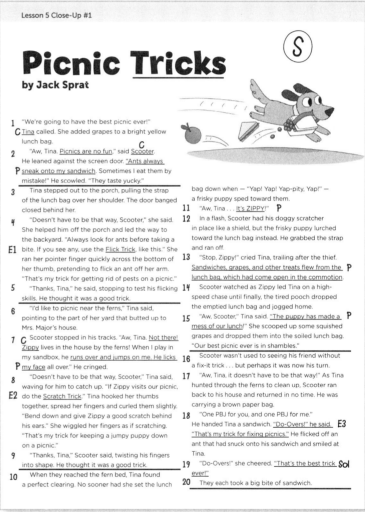

Lesson 5 Close-Up #1

Picnic Tricks

by Jack Sprat

S

1 "We're going to have the best picnic ever!" C Tina called. She added grapes to a bright yellow lunch bag.

2 "Aw, Tina. Picnics are no fun," said Scooter. He leaned against the screen door. "Ants always P sneak onto my sandwich. Sometimes I eat them by mistake!" He scowled. "They taste yucky."

3 Tina stepped out to the porch, pulling the strap of the lunch bag over her shoulder. The door banged closed behind her.

4 "Doesn't have to be that way, Scooter," she said. She helped him off the porch and led the way to the backyard. "Always look for ants before taking a E1 bite. If you see any, use the Flick Trick, like this." She ran her pointer finger quickly across the bottom of her thumb, pretending to flick an ant off her arm. "That's my trick for getting rid of pests on a picnic."

5 "Thanks, Tina," he said, stopping to test his flicking skills. He thought it was a good trick.

6 "I'd like to picnic near the ferns," Tina said, pointing to the part of her yard that butted up to Mrs. Major's house.

7 C Scooter stopped in his tracks. "Aw, Tina. Not there! Zippy lives in the house by the ferns! When I play in my sandbox, he runs over and jumps on me. He licks P my face all over." He cringed.

8 "Doesn't have to be that way, Scooter," Tina said, waving for him to catch up. "If Zippy visits our picnic, E2 do the Scratch Trick." Tina hooked her thumbs together, spread her fingers and curled them slightly. "Bend down and give Zippy a good scratch behind his ears." She wiggled her fingers as if scratching. "That's my trick for keeping a jumpy puppy down on a picnic."

9 "Thanks, Tina," Scooter said, twisting his fingers into shape. He thought it was a good trick.

10 When they reached the fern bed, Tina found a perfect clearing. No sooner had she set the lunch

bag down when — "Yap! Yap! Yap-pity, Yap!" — a frisky puppy sped toward them.

11 "Aw, Tina . . . It's ZIPPY!" P

12 In a flash, Scooter had his doggy scratcher in place like a shield, but the frisky puppy lurched toward the lunch bag instead. He grabbed the strap and ran off.

13 "Stop, Zippy!" cried Tina, trailing after the thief. Sandwiches, grapes, and other treats flew from the P lunch bag, which had come open in the commotion.

14 Scooter watched as Zippy led Tina on a high-speed chase until finally, the tired pooch dropped the emptied lunch bag and jogged home.

15 "Aw, Scooter," Tina said. "The puppy has made a P mess of our lunch!" She scooped up some squished grapes and dropped them into the soiled lunch bag. "Our best picnic ever is in shambles."

16 Scooter wasn't used to seeing his friend without a fix-it trick . . . but perhaps it was now his turn.

17 "Aw, Tina, it doesn't have to be that way!" As Tina hunted through the ferns to clean up, Scooter ran back to his house and returned in no time. He was carrying a brown paper bag.

18 "One PBJ for you, and one PBJ for me." He handed Tina a sandwich. "Do-Overs!" he said. E3 "That's my trick for fixing picnics." He flicked off an ant that had snuck onto his sandwich and smiled at Tina.

19 "Do-Overs!" she cheered. "That's the best trick Sol ever!"

20 They each took a big bite of sandwich.

(Available online.)

- First, let's read the title—with our pencils—and underline "Tricks." I think this is important. Let's be on the lookout for tricks.
- Next, let's number the paragraphs. Every indent tells us a new paragraph is beginning. This helps us keep track of our reading.
- Now, let's read the paragraphs slowly while using our pencils. We'll read section by section and go back to underline and code the things we find.

- In paragraph 1, underline "Tina" and code this *C* for character.

- In paragraph 2, underline "Picnics are no fun," and "Ants always sneak onto my sandwich." Let's code this *P* because this is the first clue that something is wrong. This may be the problem.

- In the same paragraph, underline "Scooter" and code this *C* for character.

- In paragraph 4, underline "Flick Trick" and code this *E1*. This event seems important, so this gets an *E*. We know "tricks" are key in this story, and this is the first one, so we'll mark it with a *1*.

- In paragraph 7, underline "Not there! Zippy . . . runs over and jumps on me. He licks my face" and code it *P*. The problem is getting worse.

- In the same paragraph, code "Zippy" with a *C* because he is also a character.

- In paragraph 8, there's another trick. Underline "Scratch Trick" and code this *E2*.

- Looks like the problem has exploded in section 4! There's a lot to underline in paragraphs 11, 13, and 15. Underline "It's ZIPPY!" (paragraph 11), and the whole sentence that starts "Sandwiches, grapes, and other treats . . ." (paragraph 13), and finally "The puppy has made a mess of our lunch!" (paragraph 15). Code these *P*.

- Now, we're in the last section. In paragraph 18, underline "'Do-Overs!' he said. 'That's my trick for fixing picnics.'" Code this *E3*. It's another trick.

- Finally, in paragraph 19, underline "That's the best trick ever!" and code this *Sol*, because it's the solution.

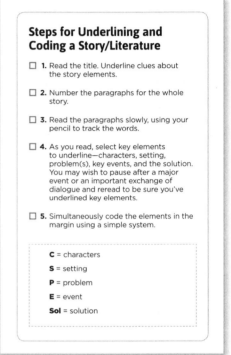

Steps for Underlining and Coding a Story/Literature

☐ **1.** Read the title. Underline clues about the story elements.

☐ **2.** Number the paragraphs for the whole story.

☐ **3.** Read the paragraphs slowly, using your pencil to track the words.

☐ **4.** As you read, select key elements to underline—characters, setting, problem(s), key events, and the solution. You may wish to pause after a major event or an important exchange of dialogue and reread to be sure you've underlined key elements.

☐ **5.** Simultaneously code the elements in the margin using a simple system.

C = characters
S = setting
P = problem
E = event
Sol = solution

(See Appendix, page 116.)

Say to students: *As you can see, underlining and coding helps us track how the story unfolds. We keep track of the characters, the events, and the problem and solution. We also feel for the characters. As they solve their problems and learn and grow, so do we. This lesson they learn is the theme, which can be stated as: "We can solve problems creatively."* Explain that while the text does not specifically state the theme, we can figure it out from the story elements.

Hand out copies of "Steps for Underlining and Coding a Story/Literature" (page 116) and discuss with the class.

Close-Up #2: When Looks Matter

Tell students: *Let's revisit "When Looks Matter," which we coded A for article, based on our prediction. Remember, we are on the lookout for the topic, key ideas in each paragraph, how the details are told, and the author's point (main idea) about the topic. Let's see how we can use text-marking to support our search. Are we ready to read with our pencils?*

Display "When Looks Matter" (page 110) on the board and hand out copies. Go over the displayed text together and have students follow along on their hard copy as you think aloud and text-mark the passage.

- First, let's read the title—with our pencils—and underline "Looks." I think this is important. Let's be on the lookout for ideas about looks.

- Next, let's number the paragraphs. Remember, every indent tells us a new paragraph is beginning. This helps us keep track of things.

- Now, we're going to read the paragraphs slowly using our pencils. We'll read section by section and go back to underline key ideas we find.

- Select words to underline that would help us give an oral summary of each paragraph.

- I think the main idea of the article is in two places. In paragraph 4, code *MI* where the author tells us the reasons animals are ugly. In paragraph 7, also code *MI* where the author tells us about caring for all animals. These are the main ideas.

Say to students: *Underlining and coding key ideas help us see how each paragraph adds something new to our understanding about the topic. Together, these ideas shape the author's central idea.*

Lesson 5 Close-Up #2

When Looks Matter (A)

Pangolins live in Africa and Asia.

1 Which animal would you rather snuggle up with—a panda cub or a blobfish? Most people would say the panda, but not scientist Lucy Cooke. She takes pictures and videos of the world's oddest-looking creatures. She wants to teach people about these animals before it's too late. Many, like the proboscis monkey, are endangered and could use a helping hand.

Animal Planet

2 There are more than 10,000 known **endangered** animal species in the world. But a recent study found that groups that protect animals usually focus on cute, cuddly creatures. Why? It's easier to convince people to help them. That's bad news for the ugly animals—and for the animals and plants around them.

Words to Know
endangered: in danger of dying out
ecosystem: a group of animals and plants that live together
predators: animals that eat other animals

Blobfish live in the deep waters surrounding Australia.

When a species dies out, its entire **ecosystem** can be harmed.

3 Every animal plays an important role in an ecosystem. Take frogs, for example. Yes, they can be slimy. But if they were to disappear, the snakes and birds that eat them could die out too. And with no frogs to gobble up bugs, the number of insects might get out of control.

Ugly for a Reason

4 Cooke says there's a good reason that animals aren't all adorable. Often the things we find weird in animals help them MI survive in the wild. She points to one of her favorite animals—the pangolin.

5 The pangolin is covered from head to tail with large, hard scales. This body armor protects it from toothy **predators** like tigers.

6 Cooke hopes that her work will make people care about all animals, no matter what they look like.

7 "Once you understand why MI they're ugly or odd," she says, "I hope you'll appreciate and want to save them as much as I do."

Proboscis (pruh-BAH-sis) monkeys live in Borneo, an island nation in Asia.

(Available online.)

Hand out copies of "Steps for Underlining and Coding Informational Text" (page 116) and discuss with the class.

 For more practice, use additional text passages in the Appendix, pages 111–114.

Quick Close

Review the lesson by asking: *How does "reading with a pencil" or text-marking help us interact effectively with a text?*

- It helps us identify and note important ideas in texts.
- Underlining the literary elements helps us follow along as a story unfolds. We develop feelings for the characters and their problems and solutions. As the characters solve their problems and learn and grow, so do we. This lesson they learn is the theme.
- Underlining and coding key ideas help us see how each paragraph adds something new to our understanding about the topic. Together, these ideas shape the author's main idea.

Steps for Underlining and Coding Informational Text

☐ **1.** Read the title. Underline clues about the topic.

☐ **2.** Number the paragraphs for the whole article.

☐ **3.** Read paragraph 1, using your pencil to track the words.

☐ **4.** Reread paragraph 1 and select key ideas to underline. As a guide, underline only key ideas that would help you present an oral summary of the paragraph.

☐ **5.** Repeat this for each paragraph.

☐ **6.** You may detect the main idea expressed in a sentence at the beginning, the end, or in the middle of the paragraph. Code it in the margin using a simple *MI*.

(See Appendix, page 116.)

Independent Readiness Survey

Gauge students' comfort level with their basic text-marking skills. Read the numbered statements below and have students respond in one of three ways:

- Thumbs up if they agree
- Thumbs down if they disagree and want more guided practice with a teacher
- Thumbs midway if they almost agree but would like to work with a partner

1. I can independently underline the story elements in a story/literature (character, setting, problem, events, solution).

2. I can independently underline key ideas in an article or informational passage.

3. I can independently code story elements or key ideas and other critical information about a text.

Teaching Notes

- Underlining and coding are very easy Text-Marking strategies to integrate into your planned instruction. Have students practice using a variety of reading passages—both literature (stories) and informational texts (articles).

- As you remind students to underline only key ideas that would help them present an oral summary of a paragraph, you may want to model how to make an oral summary.

- Encourage students to flexibly adapt the Text-Marking strategies to suit their style. Text-marking is not rigid and becomes a very unique, personal skill. While each student's paper may mimic some of the same text-markings as another's, it's not likely—nor expected—that they will ever match completely.

- Help students recognize key ideas or critical elements for text-marking to reinforce your comprehension instruction. Use teachable moments to quickly review or spotlight helpful examples that will build student understanding.

- Some students may benefit from additional guided practice to help them better gauge the effectiveness of their text-marking. The quantity of text-marking is less important than the quality; too much or too little doesn't serve the objective of aiding the reader as he or she returns to the text.

- Using color for underlining and/or coding may be helpful for some students. It may also be helpful to color-code areas to spotlight, such as where a problem in a story first begins, where it grows, and where it is solved. Color can connect ideas found in different areas in a passage and serve as reminders to students.

- Students who struggle with comprehension may need several repeated readings of a passage and/or other ways to segment texts. Repeatedly reading smaller segments of texts may be more manageable for some students.

- As students practice and gain proficiency with close reading, they may not need to reread an entire passage or sections of a passage to text-mark effectively. Instead, they learn to adjust their pace, attentiveness, and advancement based on their unique interactions with a text. Our goal is to help each student become an effective, comprehension-building text-marker—in real time.

- Extend ways to underline and code texts to enhance the effectiveness of the Text-Marking strategy. Students can use this strategy to build vocabulary, note sentence variety, bolster comprehension, and support other literacy skills useful for reading and writing.

LESSON 6

Advanced Text-Marking Strategy: Using Symbols and More Codes

Share additional text-marking symbols and codes so students can interact with the text in even more meaningful ways.

Quick Start: Text-marking is a way to interact with a text. If you could add on to the symbols and codes from Lesson 5, what would they be?

Making Connections

Ask students: *What other symbols and codes would enhance our text-marking strategy?* (Sample responses: A code for when we don't know what a word means; when we like a word; if the text makes us feel happy or sad; when something surprises us; if we don't understand something)

Explain to students that when we read, we share many kinds of interactions with texts. Why not add on key symbols and codes so we can record them, too? Review the Steps for Underlining and Coding Story/Literature and Informational Text (page 116). Ask: *What are some other symbols we can use to code our texts?* Display the "Text-Marking Add-Ons" chart (page 117) on the board and discuss with students.

Close-Up #1: Picnic Tricks

Say to students: *Remember in "Picnic Tricks" we text-marked the story elements—characters, problem, events, solution—and arrived at a theme (what the character learns). Let's add our new symbols and codes.*

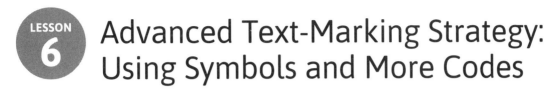

Text-Marking Add-Ons

We read with our pencils!

Circle words = unknown, interesting vocabulary words

Underline = important ideas

Box ideas = dates, numbers

Reactions to text and inner voice

? = wonderings, questions, don't understand

! = excitement, surprise

☺☹ = emotions/feelings while you read

1, 2, 3 = number paragraphs, lists, and ideas

(See Appendix, page 117.)

Display "Picnic Tricks" (page 109) on the board and hand out copies. Read through the displayed text together and have students follow along on their hard copy as you think aloud and text-mark the passage:

- I'll add a happy face in paragraph 1. Picnics make me happy.
- I'll make a sad face in paragraph 2. No one likes to eat bugs!
- In paragraph 2, I'll circle *scowled*. It's an interesting word that shows something tasted yucky.
- I'll put an exclamation point (!) next to paragraph 4. I know that trick!
- I'll make a sad face here in paragraph 7. I don't like getting licked on the face by my dog.
- In the same paragraph, I'll also circle *cringed*, which is another word to describe an "I-don't-like-that!" look.

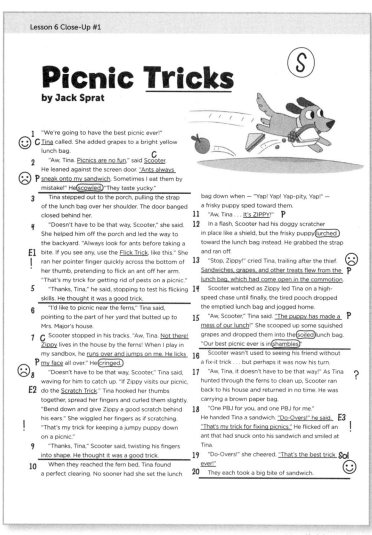

(Available online.)

- Wow, that was a good trick! I'm adding another (!) next to paragraph 8.

- I'll circle *lurched* in paragraph 12. I think it means "to jump toward," which would make sense, but I'm not sure.

- I feel bad for Tina in paragraph 13, so I'll put a sad face.

- In paragraph 15, I'll circle *soiled* and *shambles*. I think *soiled* means "got dirty," like to get soil or dirt on something. I think *shambles* means "wrecked." When I swap that out, it works.

- I wonder what Scooter is going to do. Let me put a question mark (?) next to paragraph 16.

- Oh, wow! What a great idea! I bet Tina was surprised. What a nice friend. I'm putting an (!) next to paragraph 18.

- I'll put a happy face next to the last sentence because I would feel really happy if this were me.

Tell students that adding these symbols and codes while we read helps remind us of our personal reaction to the text. Something in the text has made us feel happy, sad, or angry. Often, our feelings help us figure out the deeper meaning of a story. Here, we are happy that Scooter has saved the picnic. This kind of reaction to the text helps us grasp the theme that we can be creative problem solvers. We may also detect new things by thinking about these add-ons, like when we circle new words such as *scowled*, *cringed*, and *lurched*. Explain to students that they may have different reactions to the text so they may mark it differently than you did—and this is perfectly fine.

Close-Up #2: When Looks Matter

Say to students: *Let's revisit "When Looks Matter." Remember, we were on the lookout for the topic, key ideas in each paragraph, how the details are told, the author's point (main idea) about the topic. Let's add our new symbols and codes. Are we ready to read with our pencils?*

Display "When Looks Matter" (page 110) on the board and hand out copies. Read through the displayed text together and have students follow along on their hard copy as you think aloud and text-mark the passage:

- Thinking what it would be like to snuggle up with blobfish made me laugh, so I'll put a happy face in the margin next to paragraph 1.

- I'm going to circle *proboscis* in the same paragraph because it's an interesting word. I think it's a kind of monkey.

- I wonder what kind of helping hand. I'm going to put a (?) next to that.

- I'll place an (!) next to paragraph 2 because I was surprised that there are so many endangered animals.

- I'll add a sad face in paragraph 2 also because I'm sad that the ugly animals aren't protected in the same way as the cute animals. That seems unfair!

- In paragraph 3, I was surprised to learn about the effects a frog has on the ecosystem, so I'll put an (!) next to that paragraph.

- In paragraph 4, I'll circle *adorable* because it's a great word that I could use to replace the word *pretty*.

- I'll add a happy face in paragraph 4 because I like the idea that being an ugly animal can be a good thing— it helps the animal survive!

- I'll add an (!) at the last paragraph because now I appreciate and want to save the ugly animals!

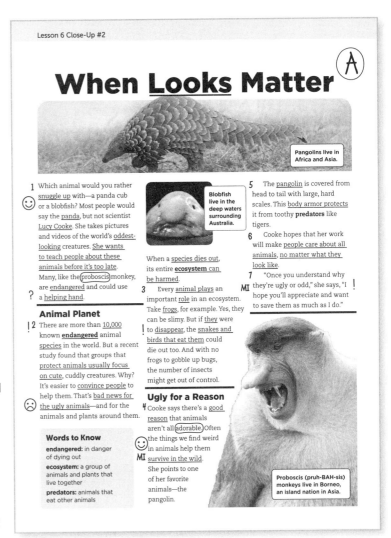

Lesson 6 Close-Up #2

When <u>Looks</u> Matter Ⓐ

Pangolins live in Africa and Asia.

1 Which animal would you rather <u>snuggle up</u> with—a panda cub ☺ or a blobfish? Most people would say the <u>panda</u>, but not scientist <u>Lucy Cooke</u>. She takes pictures and videos of the world's <u>oddest-looking</u> creatures. <u>She wants to teach people about these animals before it's too late</u>. Many, like the ⟨proboscis⟩ monkey, are <u>endangered</u> and could use ? a <u>helping hand</u>.

Animal Planet

!2 There are more than <u>10,000</u> known **endangered** animal <u>species</u> in the world. But a recent study found that groups that <u>protect animals usually focus on cute</u>, cuddly creatures. Why? It's easier to <u>convince people</u> to help them. That's <u>bad news for</u> ☹ <u>the ugly animals</u>—and for the animals and plants around them.

Blobfish live in the deep waters surrounding Australia.

When a <u>species dies out</u>, its entire **ecosystem** <u>can be harmed</u>.

3 Every <u>animal plays an</u> important <u>role</u> in an ecosystem. Take <u>frogs</u>, for example. Yes, they can be slimy. But if <u>they</u> were MI to <u>disappear</u>, the <u>snakes and birds that eat them</u> could die out too. And with no frogs to gobble up bugs, the number of insects might get out of control.

Ugly for a Reason

4 Cooke says there's a <u>good reason</u> that animals aren't all ⟨adorable⟩ Often ☺ the things we find weird in animals help them MI <u>survive in the wild</u>. She points to one of her favorite animals—the pangolin.

5 The <u>pangolin</u> is covered from head to tail with large, hard scales. This <u>body armor protects</u> it from toothy **predators** like tigers.

6 Cooke hopes that her work will make <u>people care about all animals</u>, <u>no matter what they look like</u>.

7 "Once you understand why they're ugly or odd," she says, "I ! hope you'll appreciate and want to save them as much as I do."

Proboscis (pruh-BAH-sis) monkeys live in Borneo, an island nation in Asia.

Words to Know

endangered: in danger of dying out

ecosystem: a group of animals and plants that live together

predators: animals that eat other animals

(Available online.)

Explain to students that underlining and coding key ideas helps us see how each paragraph adds something new to our understanding about the topic. Together, these ideas shape the author's main idea. Here, too, adding these new symbols and codes while we read helps remind us of our reactions to the text. Something in the text has made us feel happy, sad, or angry. Often, our feelings help us figure out the deeper meaning of an article. For example, our feelings about ugly animals may change after reading the article. We not only learn that animals may be "ugly" in order to survive, but we also want to help those ugly animals that are endangered. Our reaction to the text helps us grasp this main idea. We may also detect new things by thinking about these add-ons, such as circling new words, like *adorable*.

For more practice, use additional text passages in the Appendix, pages 111–114.

Quick Close

Say to students: *How does using these add-ons in our Text-Marking strategies help us interact effectively with a text?*

- It helps us note and track our feelings in texts, which in turn helps us identify a theme or an author's main idea.

- It helps us notice new and interesting vocabulary. By learning new words, we can build our understanding of the text. Using these new words in our own writing helps build our vocabulary.
- It helps us recognize an author's style and appreciate an author's unique ways of expressing ideas. By experimenting and using an author's style in our own writing, we can discover our own style.

Independent Readiness Survey

Gauge students' comfort level with these advanced text-marking skills. Read the numbered statements below and have students respond in one of three ways:
- Thumbs up if they agree
- Thumbs down if they disagree and want more guided practice with a teacher
- Thumbs midway if they almost agree but would like to work with a partner

1. I can independently code text with add-ons.
2. I can begin to recognize an author's writing style and decide if I'd like to try it in my own writing.
3. I can independently note my reactions to a passage and use this knowledge to build my understanding of the main idea.

Teaching Notes

- Text-marking with symbols and codes is very easy to integrate into classroom instruction. It is also easy to merge these new methods with others from Lesson 5. Both can be used with content-area instruction as well as with activities that fall within ELA.

- Encourage students to share their ideas for coding a passage out loud. This is another quick way to apply and practice this skill routinely.

- Some students may lean toward coding in a certain way. For example, some may interact emotionally (using emojis), while others may react to text structure (coding lists, boxing numbers, and so on). Have students work in pairs or small groups to help expand their understanding of many possible applications.

- Caution students from becoming overzealous with text-marking. Remind them that the objective is to mark the text purposefully and in ways that are authentic.

- While it's important to allow for flexibility with text-marking, you will also want to set expectations for some "must-see" codes. For example, an unexpected surprise (carefully crafted by an author) should be coded with an exclamation mark or in another way. Text-marking can serve as a check on student comprehension.

- It's important to keep in mind that *practicing* text-marking may not necessarily mimic *authentic* text-marking. Jockeying between guided practice and authentic application is part of the learning process. As students become proficient in recognizing ways they can note their interactions with the text, their text-marking skills align with their authentic reactions.

- Some students may benefit from working on these text-marking strategies one at a time. For example, begin by practicing with new vocabulary, and then move on to emotions.

- Be sure to create simple processes for addressing students' needs with unknown vocabulary words or if they don't understand what they've read. Incorporate the methods you use for instruction.

- Another way to scaffold students' skill development is to use premade sticky notes to help them respond to the text.

LESSON 7

Extreme Text-Marking Strategy: Using Gist Statements and Hashtags (#)

Demonstrate the more powerful techniques of writing gist statements and labeling text using hashtags. Both build comprehension and serve as location markers for a text.

Quick Start: What other ways can we mark up the text we're reading?

Making Connections

Tell students: *Text-marking is a way to note your interactions with a text. We've seen a few ways to mark text, using underlines, circles, and other codes. There are two quick and easy strategies you'll want to add to your collection: gist statements and hashtags. You would use one or the other—not both.*

Explain that the word *gist* means "the core idea or the central point or essence of something." A gist statement is a brief, fine-tuned sentence or two about a section of text. It's the "bull's-eye of meaning" about that section. In contrast, hashtags are shorter, two- or three-word labels you assign to a section of text. A hashtag sums up the content in a very short yet thoughtful way. Both are best used together with other key text-marking strategies, such as underlining, coding, and text-marking add-ons.

Say to students: *Once you've mastered the strategies, figuring out the mix and match that works best for you will come easily. Eventually, you'll develop a text-marking style that's all your own—unique! Let's take a close look.*

Close-Up #1: Picnic Tricks

Say to students: *Remember in "Picnic Tricks," we text-marked the story elements, then we added new symbols and codes. Let's revisit the story and explore writing gist statements.*

Display the gist-statements version of "Picnic Tricks" (available online) on the board and hand out copies. Point out the gist statements that have been added at the end of each section and discuss them as a class. Explain that adding the gist statements serves many purposes.

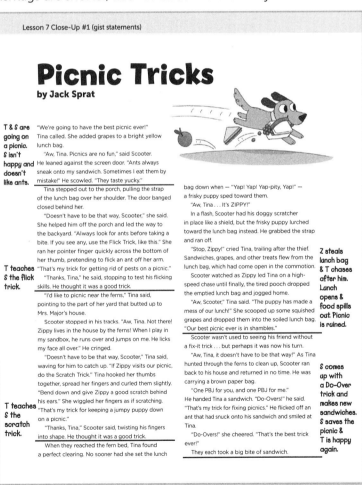

Lesson 7 Close-Up #1 (gist statements)

Picnic Tricks
by Jack Sprat

T & S are going on a picnic. S isn't happy and doesn't like ants. "We're going to have the best picnic ever!" Tina called. She added grapes to a bright yellow lunch bag.

"Aw, Tina. Picnics are no fun," said Scooter. He leaned against the screen door. "Ants always sneak onto my sandwich. Sometimes I eat them by mistake!" He scowled. "They taste yucky."

Tina stepped out to the porch, pulling the strap of the lunch bag over her shoulder. The door banged closed behind her.

"Doesn't have to be that way, Scooter," she said. She helped him off the porch and led the way to the backyard. "Always look for ants before taking a bite. If you see any, use the Flick Trick, like this." She ran her pointer finger quickly across the bottom of her thumb, pretending to flick an ant off her arm.

T teaches S the flick trick. "That's my trick for getting rid of pests on a picnic."

"Thanks, Tina," he said, stopping to test his flicking skills. He thought it was a good trick.

"I'd like to picnic near the ferns," Tina said, pointing to the part of her yard that butted up to Mrs. Major's house.

Scooter stopped in his tracks. "Aw, Tina. Not there! Zippy lives in the house by the ferns! When I play in my sandbox, he runs over and jumps on me. He licks my face all over." He cringed.

"Doesn't have to be that way, Scooter," Tina said, waving for him to catch up. "If Zippy visits our picnic, do the Scratch Trick." Tina hooked her thumbs together, spread her fingers and curled them slightly. "Bend down and give Zippy a good scratch behind his ears." She wiggled her fingers as if scratching.

T teaches S the scratch trick. "That's my trick for keeping a jumpy puppy down on a picnic."

"Thanks, Tina," Scooter said, twisting his fingers into shape. He thought it was a good trick.

When they reached the fern bed, Tina found a perfect clearing. No sooner had she set the lunch bag down when — "Yap! Yap! Yap-pity, Yap!" — a frisky puppy sped toward them.

"Aw, Tina . . . It's ZIPPY!"

In a flash, Scooter had his doggy scratcher in place like a shield, but the frisky puppy lurched toward the lunch bag instead. He grabbed the strap and ran off.

"Stop, Zippy!" cried Tina, trailing after the thief. Sandwiches, grapes, and other treats flew from the lunch bag, which had come open in the commotion.

Z steals lunch bag & T chases after him. Lunch opens & food spills out. Picnic is ruined. Scooter watched as Zippy led Tina on a high-speed chase until finally, the tired pooch dropped the emptied lunch bag and jogged home.

"Aw, Scooter," Tina said. "The puppy has made a mess of our lunch!" She scooped up some squished grapes and dropped them into the soiled lunch bag. "Our best picnic ever is in shambles."

Scooter wasn't used to seeing his friend without a fix-it trick . . . but perhaps it was now his turn.

"Aw, Tina, it doesn't have to be that way!" As Tina hunted through the ferns to clean up, Scooter ran back to his house and returned in no time. He was carrying a brown paper bag.

S comes up with a Do-Over trick and makes new sandwiches. S saves the picnic & T is happy again. "One PBJ for you, and one PBJ for me." He handed Tina a sandwich. "Do-Overs!" he said. "That's my trick for fixing picnics." He flicked off an ant that had snuck onto his sandwich and smiled at Tina.

"Do-Overs!" she cheered. "That's the best trick ever!"

They each took a big bite of sandwich.

(Available online.)

- It confirms our understanding of each section of text.
- It helps us fuse our multiple mini understandings together into a larger, more meaningful understanding of the entire passage.
- It helps us remember the text and reminds us where information is located so we can quickly return to it, if necessary.

Lesson 7 Close-Up #1 (hashtags)

Picnic Tricks
by Jack Sprat

"We're going to have the best picnic ever!" Tina called. She added grapes to a bright yellow lunch bag.

"Aw, Tina. Picnics are no fun," said Scooter. He leaned against the screen door. "Ants always sneak onto my sandwich. Sometimes I eat them by mistake!" He scowled. "They taste yucky."

#picnic problems

Tina stepped out to the porch, pulling the strap of the lunch bag over her shoulder. The door banged closed behind her.

"Doesn't have to be that way, Scooter," she said. She helped him off the porch and led the way to the backyard. "Always look for ants before taking a bite. If you see any, use the Flick Trick, like this." She ran her pointer finger quickly across the bottom of her thumb, pretending to flick an ant off her arm. "That's my trick for getting rid of pests on a picnic."

#flick trick

"Thanks, Tina," he said, stopping to test his flicking skills. He thought it was a good trick.

"I'd like to picnic near the ferns," Tina said, pointing to the part of her yard that butted up to Mrs. Major's house.

Scooter stopped in his tracks. "Aw, Tina. Not there! Zippy lives in the house by the ferns! When I play in my sandbox, he runs over and jumps on me. He licks my face all over." He cringed.

"Doesn't have to be that way, Scooter," Tina said, waving for him to catch up. "If Zippy visits our picnic, do the Scratch Trick." Tina hooked her thumbs together, spread her fingers and curled them slightly. "Bend down and give Zippy a good scratch behind his ears." She wiggled her fingers as if scratching. "That's my trick for keeping a jumpy puppy down on a picnic."

#scratch trick

"Thanks, Tina," Scooter said, twisting his fingers into shape. He thought it was a good trick.

When they reached the fern bed, Tina found a perfect clearing. No sooner had she set the lunch bag down when — "Yap! Yap! Yap-pity, Yap!" — a frisky puppy sped toward them.

"Aw, Tina . . . It's ZIPPY!"

In a flash, Scooter had his doggy scratcher in place like a shield, but the frisky puppy lurched toward the lunch bag instead. He grabbed the strap and ran off.

"Stop, Zippy!" cried Tina, trailing after the thief. Sandwiches, grapes, and other treats flew from the lunch bag, which had come open in the commotion.

Scooter watched as Zippy led Tina on a high-speed chase until finally, the tired pooch dropped the emptied lunch bag and jogged home.

"Aw, Scooter," Tina said. "The puppy has made a mess of our lunch!" She scooped up some squished grapes and dropped them into the soiled lunch bag. "Our best picnic ever is in shambles."

#picnic in shambles

Scooter wasn't used to seeing his friend without a fix-it trick . . . but perhaps it was now his turn.

"Aw, Tina, it doesn't have to be that way!" As Tina hunted through the ferns to clean up, Scooter ran back to his house and returned in no time. He was carrying a brown paper bag.

"One PBJ for you, and one PBJ for me." He handed Tina a sandwich. "Do-Overs!" he said. "That's my trick for fixing picnics." He flicked off an ant that had snuck onto his sandwich and smiled at Tina.

"Do-Overs!" she cheered. "That's the best trick ever!"

They each took a big bite of sandwich.

#Do-Over

(Available online.)

Next, display the hashtag version of "Picnic Tricks" (available online) on the board and hand out copies. Say to students: *Now, let's move to hashtags. It's easy to see the difference between hashtags and gist statements. Hashtags streamline our text-marking process. They're most useful after we practice, improve, and get better at close reading and text-marking passages.* Discuss the hashtags in each section, inviting students to offer suggestions for alternative words or phrases.

Guide students to notice that we still continue to read with intent and purpose, to look for elements, and to think carefully about our feelings. Only now, our hashtags trigger our deep-level thinking, which we can recall as needed. They also tag the location where specific content is located should we need to return and review the text.

Close-Up #2: When Looks Matter

Say: *Let's revisit "When Looks Matter." Remember that we were on the lookout for the topic, the key ideas, how details were told, and the author's main idea about the topic. Then later, we added new symbols and codes. Let's revisit this passage and explore writing gist statements.*

Display the gist version of "When Looks Matter" (available online) on the board and hand out copies. Point out the gist statements that have been added next to each paragraph and discuss them as a class. Say: *Adding gist statements to informational text serves similar purposes as in stories.*

- It confirms our understanding of each paragraph in the text.
- It helps us fuse our multiple mini understandings together into a larger, more meaningful understanding of the entire passage.
- It helps us remember the text and reminds us where information is located so we can quickly return to it, if necessary.

Next, display the hashtag version of "When Looks Matter" (available online) on the board and hand out copies. Say to students: *Now, let's move on to hashtags. Here, too, it's easy to see the difference between hashtags and gist statements. Hashtags streamline our text-marking process. They're most useful after we practice, improve, and get better at close reading and text-marking passages.* Discuss the hashtags after each paragraph, inviting students to offer suggestions for alternative words or phrases.

Explain that just as with the previous fictional passage, we continue to read with intent and purpose, we look for elements, and we continue to think carefully about our feelings. Similarly, our hashtags trigger our deep-level thinking, which we can recall as needed. In addition, they tag the location where specific content is located should we need to return and review the text.

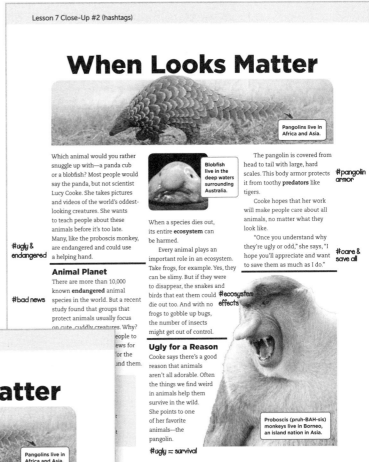

(Available online.)

(Available online.)

For more practice, use additional text passages in the Appendix, pages 111–114.

Quick Close

Explain to students that when used together with other text-marking strategies, gist statements and hashtags help us dig more deeply into a text passage. We focus on key events, and we think about how they make us feel. Finally, we build our knowledge about stories and articles. We understand how an author welcomes us into the story by making us care about a character or a topic. We also value the takeaways from the text passage, such as a new understanding of a simple life lesson and/or an improved vocabulary.

Independent Readiness Survey

Gauge students' comfort level with using gist statements and hashtags. Read the numbered statements below and have students respond in one of three ways:

- Thumbs up if they agree
- Thumbs down if they disagree and want more guided practice with a teacher
- Thumbs midway if they almost agree but would like to work with a partner

1. I understand how to write gist statements for a passage.
2. I understand how to label a passage with hashtags.
3. I understand how to effectively use these text-marking strategies with some of the others I've learned—to build and confirm my understanding and to return to locations in the text as needed.

Teaching Notes

- Students can work with the keywords and phrases they've underlined to write gist statements or hashtags. Modeling how to connect the words and phrases in a brief, written summary style should mimic the process for rehearsing an oral summary.

- One way to section nonfiction is to use paragraphs. Students readily grasp that each paragraph contributes something new to the topic. (Group two or three paragraphs together when it makes sense to do so.) The gist statement should reflect the unique content. Modeling, guiding and monitoring, and independent practice are necessary for all students.

- One way to section and hashtag a fictional piece is when an event or a character's feeling shifts or when a character's actions fail or succeed. You may need to model this for students and then guide and monitor them as needed as they practice independently. To practice with students, read aloud a passage and pause, saying, "Hashtag here." Over time, students will recognize important shifts.

- Students can abbreviate names, places, and so on, in their gist statements. They can use symbols to abbreviate, too. If they need to access the full information (such as when writing a response), they can easily return to the passage.

- Hashtags are best reserved as a finale of Text-Marking strategies.

- Each section must be labeled differently. Tell students they can return to and change a hashtag label. Remember, hashtags are short, but thoughtful. Have them refine their # label as necessary to make it more precise and unique to that section. This reflects careful thinking.

CHAPTER 2

Quick & Easy Strategies for Writing Short Responses

Do your students have a plan for writing an effective short response? Short-response questions typically ask students to demonstrate—in writing—their understanding of crucial elements of a text passage they have read. In other words, they ask students to show and share with others their thinking and text-based analysis. Short-response questions may probe understanding of key ideas and details in the passage or the author's use of craft and structure. They may refer to an entire passage or to specific paragraphs or sections. They may also require different levels of thinking and analysis.

Despite these variables, all of the questions will require a written response that includes original thinking and text-based evidence as support. While it goes without saying that effective close-reading strategies, such as those shared in the last chapter, help students with their response writing, there's more to it than that.

Buzz & Chatter

Short-Response vs. Extended-Response Questions

It is worth noting that there is a great difference between short- and extended-response questions—much more than the amount of space provided for a response and the amount of points that can be awarded. A short response must often include an inference and at least two supporting details, according to most standards-based grading rubrics. (See Figure 4, next page.) An inference can be described as an interpretation, presumption, or way of thinking that stems from suggestions found in a text. Teachers often describe this complex skill as "reading between the lines." This is difficult for many students. What makes the short response particularly challenging is that students must unpack their inferential thinking and evidence-based explanation in a short amount of space in order to receive full credit. This requires a level of precision that many elementary-level writers are still developing.

2-Point Rubric

FIGURE 4

Score	Response Features
2 points	The features of a 2-point response are: • valid inferences and/or claims from the text where required by the prompt • evidence of analysis of the text where required by the prompt • relevant facts, definitions, concrete details, and/or other information from the text to develop response according to the requirements of the prompt • sufficient number of facts, definitions, concrete details, and/or other information from the text as required by the prompt • complete sentences where errors do not impact readability

No doubt some students are inherently good at writing short answers. Their ideas are spot on, and their thinking flows in a straight line like an arrow to a bull's-eye. They are also effective communicators, making it easy for us to follow along when they share their ideas in writing. These young, skilled thinker-writers are a marvel! Yet, most of our students are not there . . . yet. Instead, they are still developing this complex thinking-writing skill and can benefit from our help. This is especially true because short-response writing bypasses the traditional writing process and its gradual and recursive developmental cycle. We need to devise an alternative process that can help students answer questions in real time.

An Alternative Writing Process: The RACE Strategy

The greatest way to help students with short responses is to provide them with a plan that guides and supports their good thinking and good writing—a type of alternative writing-process approach—that is timely, efficient, and useful. The RACE strategy is such a plan.

RACE is an acronym—a form of mnemonic device used to help students remember different kinds of information, such as the names of the Great Lakes (HOMES: Huron, Ontario, Michigan, Erie, and Superior) or capitalization rules (MINTS: Months, the letter *I*, Names, Titles, and Start of a sentence). In this case, RACE serves as a reminder to students of the key how-to's of response writing. The letters stand for:

R = Restate
A = Answer (or infer)
C = Cite evidence
E = Edit

The acronym makes the content and structure—or the must-haves—of response writing transparent. It suggests a flexible checklist and plan for students to guide their thinking and their written response. Figure 5 (next page) draws the parallels between the must-haves of a short response and the acronym reminder to guide students' thinking and writing.

FIGURE 5

Must-Haves to Include in a Short Response (per most standards-based rubrics)	RACE strategy (a thinking-writing routine)
• address the task	**R** = restate
• students' original ideas	**A** = answer/inference
• include text evidence in support of students' ideas	**C** = cite evidence
• show organization and command of grade-level written skill	**E** = edit

Certainly, there are other acronyms that can serve as helpful reminders to student writers. There are also ways to reshape the acronym so it is more grade-level friendly. For example, Figure 6 (below) shows one district's approach to using slightly different response-writing acronyms in Grades 3 through 6. This provides some continuity as students move from one grade level to the next, but it also expands and elevates the represented skills while also aligning with growing grade-level standards and expectations. For example, 3rd-grade students work with the acronym RADDE instead of RACE, as the emphasis on their instruction is to locate two details that support a response. This changes in 4th grade, in which the term "cite evidence" more accurately reflects state standards. Likewise, the first E in 5th and 6th grades emphasizes the need to explain the relationship between the evidence and the "best" evidence.

Another way to differentiate the use of this strategy is to frame the expectations in terms of the beginning of the year versus the end of the year. For example, students new to 4th grade will transition over time into using the 4th-grade acronym and skills, students new to 5th grade will transition into using the 5th-grade acronym and skills, and so on. By the end of the year, most students are expected to demonstrate proficiency at grade level. Of course, there are exceptions, such as when student needs are met through further differentiation. In such cases, grade-level expectations could shift.

FIGURE 6

3rd Grade	4th Grade	5th Grade	6th Grade
R = restate A = answer/inference D = detail D = detail	R = restate A = answer/inference C = cite evidence (two details)	R = restate A = answer/inference C = cite best evidence E = explain	A = answer/inference C = cite best evidence E = explain
E = edit	E = explain/edit	E = edit	D = debrief (review entire answer and edit)

While this resource uses the RACE acronym and some grade-level variations, you may fine-tune it anyway that works for you and your students—or devise another acronym altogether that aligns with your grade-level standards, district initiatives, or other objectives. The processes and examples used in the lessons within this chapter (and the next) will remain helpful regardless of which acronym you choose to use.

RACE Strategy Lesson

The first lesson in this chapter introduces students to the RACE strategy. They learn of various ways they can use it to help guide their thinking, organizing, and writing. The Close-Up scaffolds show them how to apply the strategy.

Other Quick & Easy Strategies

Other powerful strategies in this chapter help students tackle each step of the RACE response.

- **Question-Attack strategies** in Lesson 9 help students understand questions by breaking them down into smaller, more manageable, and focused tasks. This process also helps students **restate (R)** the question and maximize use of the words and phrases in the question in order to target their **answer (A)**.

- **Inference-building strategies** in Lesson 10, also taught within the R and A steps of RACE, strengthen students' ability to draw and support their inferences. As mentioned earlier, an inference can be described as an interpretation, presumption, or way of thinking based on suggestions within a text, also referred to as "reading between the lines." Inferring something about any number of matters within a text—a character's motives, what causes a problem, the importance of events—is very challenging for many students, especially those who are reading at a literal or surface level. Still, helping students advance in their ability to read deeply, draw and support inferences, and communicate their ideas effectively in writing is valuable—and not only for test-taking. If tracked forward, this skill is the glimmer of what will become a student's thesis statement or an argumentative claim. Beyond that, it also welcomes, engages, and maintains a reader's interest through to the end of any text. Reading and interacting with text between the lines begins with such a glimmer!

- **Evidence-building strategies** in Lesson 11 teach students how to find, weigh, and **cite evidence (C)**. Students use their text-marking annotations to locate "hot spots" of evidence. They learn how to quote from the text, summarize, paraphrase, or use a mixture of text evidence. Guidelines help them weigh the strength of their evidence.

- **Editing strategies (E)** in Lesson 12 make use of another easy-to-remember acronym—CUPS. This reminds students what to look for during a real-time editing stage: Capitalization, Understanding, Punctuation, and Spelling. Here, too, you may wish to fine-tune the acronym in a way that works for you or devise another altogether that better aligns with your initiatives or objectives. For example, shifting the U from "understanding" to "usage" at higher grade levels is one way to differentiate and elevate the skill (see Figure 7 below). The latter implies that students should have a greater command of language arts skills than the former, which suggests a more basic grasp.

Editing & Proofreading   FIGURE 7

Grades K – mid 3	Grades mid 3 – 4+
C = capitalization	C = capitalization
U = understanding	U = usage
P = punctuation	P = punctuation
S = spelling	S = spelling

Recapping the Benefits of Short-Response Writing Strategies

RACE represents the steps skilled thinker-writers do authentically. The RACE strategy makes the structure of response writing transparent by breaking it down into small, manageable steps. It also serves as a guide to help student "think through" their ideas—from start to finish. Located within the RACE strategy are other helpful strategies: Question-Attack, inference-building, evidence-building, and editing strategies. These are used within the different stages of RACE to help students demonstrate their thinking in writing.

Buzz & Chatter

Computer-Based Testing & Short Responses

Students will rely on the close reading, Text-Marking, and Jump-Start strategies shared in earlier lessons to help them with their short responses. As mentioned in Chapter 1, they can easily apply (with some improvising) the CBT tools available to them to help with the reading component of their short-response task.

They can also easily add the RACE acronym alongside or embed it within their written response. This can be done in several ways:

1. Add in-line as students address each component – (RA) (C1) (C2) and (E)
2. Add at the beginning of their response (RACE)
3. Insert and open as needed

Again, there are ample ways students can make use of the CBT tools to meet the objectives of these helpful strategies.

Making inferences and claims—a key expectation by many states—may take some finesse. Some of the methods shared in Lesson 10 use a simply sketched graphic organizer, referred to as a grid, to help with this deeper-level thinking process. Students fill in the grid with quick notes that capture their thoughts and ideas. The objective of the grid is to make their thinking transparent and thus easier to shape, sharpen, and track. While devising this grid with CBT tools may be tricky, with practice students can improvise with the note-taking tool or insertion tool, should they continue to benefit from "seeing" their thinking.

As is true with all scaffolds, the intent is that they be removed when students don't need them anymore, when they have mastered the process. While the timing for this level of mastery is uncertain, what is certain is that we must strive to build skill with the process—and not the tool. The tools will continue to change.

The same is true with the Question-Attack skills in Lesson 9. The Question-Attack strategies, which call for students to actively mark and code questions, are no longer needed once they have mastered an ability to deeply understand what questions are asking. This comes with guided instruction and practice. Rather than circle or underline key elements of a question to analyze, a simple highlight—if that—may be all that remains necessary.

LESSON 8
Introducing the RACE Strategy for Short-Response Writing

Explore how the RACE strategy is useful as a real-time writing process plan to help students answer a variety of questions about fiction and nonfiction passages.

Quick Start: What is your plan for writing a short response?

Making Connections

Tell students: *You've read a passage carefully, using close-reading strategies. Now, you must answer a short-response question. What's your plan? Wouldn't a plan that guided you through the thinking and writing process be helpful? Introducing the RACE approach! RACE is an acronym. It stands for Restate, Answer, Cite Evidence, and Edit. Let's take a close look!*

Think & Discuss: How to Apply the RACE Strategy to Short Responses

R = restate **A** = answer **C** = cite evidence **E** = edit	The RACE strategy helps us remember what we need to include in a short response. A review of your state assessment rubric or your district writing rubric will likely include these key elements.

Humpty Dumpty

1 Humpty Dumpty sat on a wall.
2 Humpty Dumpty had a great <u>fall</u>. # fell
3 All the <u>King's horses</u> and all the <u>King's men</u>
4 Couldn't put Humpty Dumpty <u>together</u> again.

#unable to fix

1 What happened to Humpty Dumpty?
Use two details to support your response.

(RA) What happened to Humpty Dumpty was he broke into pieces and had a very bad day!

(C1) I know this because in lines 1 and 2, I learned he "sat on a wall" but then fell off.

(C2) Next, in lines 3 and 4, I learned he couldn't be put back together by the King's men.

(E) After writing your answer, read it over carefully for accuracy.

💬 Comments
1. The restate and answer (RA) are shown together. I began by restating, using words from the question to start my answer. Then, I answered using my own thoughts and my own words.
2. In (C1) and (C2), I included my evidence (referred to as "details" in the question) from the text. I even added the line numbers where I found evidence in the passage. Also, I used C1 and C2 because I had to include two details to support my answer.
3. The (E) stands for Edit. This reminds me to proofread and check for accuracy.

Close-Up #1: Humpty Dumpty

Display "Humpty Dumpty" (page 118) on the board, covering the questions on the page. Say to students: *Let's begin with an easy-to-read nursery rhyme so we can see how to use our RACE strategy as a plan to write a short response. We'll close-read and do some simple text-marking together. Then we'll answer our short-response question. Our question is:* What happened to Humpty Dumpty?

Read aloud the rhyme and number each line. Then invite students to underline keywords and add hashtags where needed (see thumbnail, left). Next, display question #1 and hand out copies. Remind students that using "details to support" a response is the same as "finding evidence."

(Available online.)

Show students how to add the *RACE* letters—almost as a checklist—to their response area, as shown on previous page. Tell students they can use *C1* and *C2* as a reminder to use two details. Say: *The RACE strategy reminds us to include everything we need in our answer. It also helps us put things in an easy-to-follow order. Gauging where to place the letters is less important than simply having them in place as a visual clue.*

If you want, share the sample response (available online) with students along with the comments and discuss as a class.

Close-Up #2:
An Extreme Adventure

Display "An Extreme Adventure" (page 119) on the board and hand out copies of the article. Say to students: *Let's try a more challenging text passage. Here's "An Extreme Adventure," which we will close-read and text-mark with hashtags and underlines. Then we'll practice the RACE strategy. The question for this story is about main idea, but only for a section of the text rather than the entire passage.*

Read the text together, then ask students to use the Jump-Start and Text-Marking strategies to identify whether the passage is fact (article) or fiction (story) and to underline keywords and add hashtags where needed (see thumbnail, top right).

Next, display question #1 (page 120) on the board and hand out copies. Tell students that when a question refers to a specific section of text, such as paragraphs or lines, it helps to mark that section by circling, boxing, or enclosing it in another manner. This also works for features,

(Available online.)

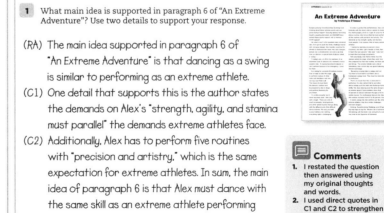

(Available online.)

such as charts, maps, or illustrations, and for parts of a manuscript, such as an introduction, footnote, or sidebar. Have students mark their response area with the letters *RACE* to remind them what they need to include in their answer. If you wish, give students a few minutes to write their responses.

Afterward, share the sample response (available online) with students and discuss using the comments to guide your discussion. Point out that the response includes a conclusion: "*In sum, the main idea . . .*" While this is a part of a well-written paragraph, students may wish to first show their ability to use evidence effectively, which is a critical requirement of a short response. Adding a fine-tuned conclusion is an excellent way to extend student response-writing skills.

Quick Close

Say to students: *The RACE strategy is a useful writing plan. It reminds us about what to include in our short responses and how to organize our ideas. It works well with a lot of different kinds of questions and with different kinds of passages. Finally, it works very well together with close-reading and text-marking strategies. Using our close-reading and text-marking strategies together with the RACE strategy is powerful!*

Independent Readiness Survey

Gauge students' comfort level with using the RACE strategy for short responses. Read the numbered statements below and have students respond in one of three ways:

- Thumbs up if they agree
- Thumbs down if they disagree and want more guided practice with a teacher
- Thumbs midway if they almost agree but would like to work with a partner

1. I know what the RACE letters stand for.
2. I know the strategy helps remind me about what to include in a short response and in what order I might want to express my ideas.
3. I can independently use the RACE strategy to help guide my original thinking, include text evidence to support my ideas, and edit my work.

Teaching Notes

- Short-response questions ask students to draw conclusions, make inferences, and/or express their original thinking about their reading—all of which can be tricky. Practicing short-response writing with the RACE strategy is most helpful using guided instruction: model, scaffold, independent application, and continuous teacher monitoring. Deep, meaningful instruction is better than vast repetitive practice.

- You may wish to discuss the differences between a short and an extended response with students. While the RACE acronym can be helpful for both (as we will see in Chapter 3), the expectations for a short response are often different than those for an extended response, according to state assessment rubrics and many district rubrics.

- The amount of space provided on a state assessment is a helpful indicator of the amount of writing expected from students. However, within that space, it is assumed that responses will be targeted and concise. Some students may need more space to express their ideas completely. As a general rule of thumb, tell students they should limit their answer so it doesn't extend beyond three written lines below the provided space. This helps prevent rambling answers and a drain on stamina.

- Remind students that the RACE strategy is flexible—there is no single right answer. It is important to build students' skill and confidence. You can best achieve this during discussions and through teacher modeling. Evidence-based thinking can often support multiple answers.

- The RACE strategy is best used with the close-reading strategies presented in Chapter 1. Using the skill sets together helps ensure that students deeply understand the text they are reading prior to answering questions. Some students may need additional support. Provide modeling, scaffolds, and ongoing monitoring.

Question-Attack Strategies for Understanding, Restating, and Answering Questions

Help students understand what a question is asking by "attacking" or unpacking it into smaller, easy-to-grasp tasks. Restating a question is a quick and easy way to begin and target a response.

Quick Start: When faced with a question, do you understand exactly what it's asking? How do you restate the question in your answer?

Making Connections

Explain to students that before they write an answer to a short-response question, they want to make sure they understand what it's asking. Question-Attack strategies are simple ways to help them "close read" a question. They can even use some of the text-marking strategies they already know. Restating the question helps them get started when they answer a short-response question. *Restating* means using some of the words from the question in their answer.

Display the "Question-Attack Strategies Checklist" (page 121) on the board and hand out copies. Go over each step with the class.

(See Appendix, page 121.)

Close-Up #1: Humpty Dumpty

Display "Humpty Dumpty" (page 118) on the board, covering the questions on the page, and review your text-markings with students. Then display question #2 and hand out copies. Model how to use the Question-Attack strategies by marking the question while thinking aloud. Have students follow along on their copies.

2 At the <u>beginning</u> of the nursery rhyme, <u>Humpty Dumpty decides to sit on a wall.</u> Why was this decision <u>unwise</u>? Use two details from the story to support your answer.

Humpty Dumpty

Humpty Dumpty sat on a wall.
Humpty Dumpty had a great fall.
All the King's horses and all the King's men
Couldn't put Humpty Dumpty together again.

(RA) Humpty's decision to sit on the wall was unwise because it was not a safe place for him.

(C1) I know this because in line 2, he had a "great fall" off the wall, which tells me he didn't think his action through very carefully. Why would an egg sit where it could have a great fall?

(C2) Also, in lines 3 and 4, Humpty "couldn't be put back together." This shows he couldn't get any do-overs on his decision—not very smart!

(E) Edit reminder

 Comments

1. I found my evidence/details to answer the question and will put a star in the margin.
2. Now I'll put my RACE reminder in the margins of my answer.
3. I'm ready to restate the question. Restating this question without making changes would sound like this: "This decision was unwise because . . ." This sounds incomplete and doesn't flow as smoothly as I'd like. I'm going to make a few changes: "Humpty's decision to sit on the wall was unwise because . . ." sounds better.

(Available online.)

- This is a long task (or question). Let's circle the question mark and trace back to the word *Why* and box it. This is a *why* question: *Why was this decision unwise?* I know I must use the word *because* in my answer to explain.

- Let's underline the location word *beginning* to remind us that this happened early in the passage.

- Let's also underline "Humpty Dumpty" because he is the subject—who this question is about.

- Underline "decides to sit on a wall" because this has the verb— the action this question is about.

- Let's also underline the word *unwise* because this is a key part of the question.

Restating the Question Checklist

When it comes to restating the question, there are three levels of skill building. These levels are based on the kinds of changes you may need to do to construct a smooth-sounding beginning. Whisper-read your writing as you start your response to help you make decisions about how to restate the question.

☐ **Simple** Nothing needs to be done to make the restated section flow smoothly.

☐ **Average** Only a few changes are needed to make the restated section flow smoothly. Changes could include:
- streamlining and omitting part of the question.
- swapping words in the question to make the meaning clear.
- reworking a clumsy-sounding sentence.

☐ **Challenging** A lot of shaping and restructuring is needed to make the restated sentence flow smoothly. You may have to:
- restructure several areas of the question.
- use two or more sentences to express complex ideas.
- use words from the question in other ways, such as at the end of your answer instead of at the beginning.

Point out to students how the Question-Attack strategy helps us focus on the question. We separate the question from the sentence that comes before and the instructions that follow. The next step is to review the passage for evidence that shows why Humpty's decision was unwise.

Afterward, display the "Restating the Question Checklist" (page 122) and discuss the different levels of changes that may need to be done to make the RA (restate/answer) part of the response sound smooth. Then display question #2 of "Humpty Dumpty" with the sample response (available online).

Students may rate the skill-building level needed to restate this question as "average"—just a few changes are necessary to improve the flow. Say: *When we restate the task, we can add words to make our sentence clear and fluent.*

(See Appendix, page 122.)

Close-Up #2: An Extreme Adventure

Say: *Let's see how we do with our Question-Attack and restating strategies in "An Extreme Adventure."* Display "An Extreme Adventure" (page 119) then question #2 (page 120) on the board and hand out copies. Model the Question-Attack strategies by marking the question while thinking aloud. Have students follow along on their copies.

- Using our Question-Attack strategies, we can see this is a "why" question . . . but it's a little unclear.

- It's asking if the introduction is effective. Let's underline that. *Effective* means something does what it's supposed to, but we have to apply our understanding to introductions.

- From our classroom writing lessons, we learned that introductions should introduce a topic in an engaging way. This question seems to ask about the craft of the introduction in this article.

- Let's go back to the passage, review the introduction, and build some evidence to write about how it introduces the topic in an engaging way.

(Available online.)

Point out how the Question-Attack strategies help us determine that we have to apply what we know about writing to answer the question. If we think about the way we write—sometimes called the "craft of writing"—the sentence makes sense (especially after we go back to the passage and notice how the author got us interested in the article).

Display question #2 of "An Extreme Adventure" with the sample response (available online). Say: *The restating is pretty simple. We want to think carefully about how to express our C1 and C2 ideas because writing about writing—which is a question about craft—can be tricky. We don't want to write vague or unfocused responses, which is a common problem with craft questions.*

This example shows how students can strengthen their "working understanding" of the question. Applying their knowledge of the craft of writing to a question can build confidence that their understanding makes sense and therefore works.

Quick Close

Explain that the Question-Attack and restating strategies help us understand the question and launch our response. They help us apply reading strategies, such as using context clues to figure out the meaning of unknown words, and make sense of the question. They help us apply what we know about words, such as thinking of words that seem related to an unknown word. They also help us apply what we know in other areas, such as writing to reading, which is very helpful when we have questions about the craft of writing. Restating helps us get off to a targeted start. It also helps us listen to the flow of our beginning idea.

Independent Readiness Survey

Gauge students' comfort level with using the Question-Attack and restating strategies for short responses. Read the numbered statements below and have students respond in one of three ways:

- Thumbs up if they agree
- Thumbs down if they disagree and want more guided practice with a teacher
- Thumbs midway if they almost agree but would like to work with a partner

1. I know how to mark short-response questions using the Question-Attack strategies.
2. I know how to restate a question (and make changes, if necessary) to help begin my short-response answer.
3. I can independently use both Question-Attack and restating strategies together to help me write clear and concise answers.

Teaching Notes

- Younger students can practice restating skills by moving words around on computer applications.

- Whisper-reading is a great mini-strategy that helps students "hear" the fluency of their sentences. It helps them shuffle and place words as they restate a question. It also helps them hear if their written answers are clear and express what they mean to say.

- Use the Speak app on computers to read back responses to help students hear the fluency of their responses.

- Students begin to develop their own original ideas, inferences, claims, and arguments as they answer questions in their own words.

- As students practice making inferences (in the following lesson), they often get tripped up and squeeze all of their ideas in one sentence. Remind them that the structure of the RA (restate/answer) calls for a broad idea.

LESSON 10 Strategies for Making Inferences and Claims

Guide students to discover effective ways to read between and beyond the lines while building their own original thinking.

Quick Start: How do you show your good thinking through inferences and claims?

Making Connections

Explain to students that as we read a passage, we piece together ideas and information from the text to build our understanding. As we do this, we also add our own ideas because an author doesn't always tell us everything. This is often called "reading between the lines" and also "reading *beyond* the lines." When we use our good thinking and come up with our own ideas, we make an inference or a claim. Both are based on evidence we've read in a passage. Ask: *What is your experience with reading between or beyond the lines (or with making an inference or a claim) in your daily activities at home or at school? Let's look at a couple of examples.*

Experience	Inference or Claim
If we have a busy Saturday with sports activities, music lessons, and visits to grandparents . . .	. . . then it's a sure thing we'll get take-out pizza for dinner because there's no time to plan and prepare meals.
If my little brother shouts, "Not again, Skippy!" while holding up his torn and tattered sneaker . . .	. . . then I know our dog Skippy has chewed up one of his sneakers again!

Tell students that when they answer short-response questions, they should include their inference or claim in their answer. It's a way to show their good thinking, their own ideas. They should also include evidence, which are the details that help them come up with their own thoughtful ideas and inferences.

Share "Ingredients of an Inference" (below) with the class and discuss.

 Think & Discuss: Ingredients of an Inference

- **A sprinkle of background knowledge.** We experience and understand many of the same things as our classmates and friends. We use this shared know-how when we read. Sometimes authors don't need to tell us everything.

- **A dash of reading between and beyond the lines.** We can also piece together our understanding from things we learn elsewhere in a story or a passage. Sometimes authors don't tell us everything but give us clues.

- **A pinch of text evidence.** Even though we can use our background knowledge and read between and beyond the lines, we still must support our ideas with solid text evidence.

(See Appendix, page 122.)

Close-Up #1: Humpty-Dumpty & Little Boy Blue

Say to students: *Let's look at two simple examples of how we read between and beyond the lines to make an inference. We'll begin with "Humpty Dumpty" and then look at "Little Boy Blue."*

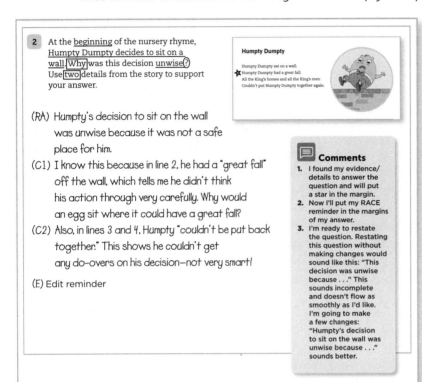

2 At the <u>beginning</u> of the nursery rhyme, <u>Humpty Dumpty decides to sit on a wall.</u> Why was this decision <u>unwise</u>? Use two details from the story to support your answer.

(RA) Humpty's decision to sit on the wall was unwise because it was not a safe place for him.

(C1) I know this because in line 2, he had a "great fall" off the wall, which tells me he didn't think his action through very carefully. Why would an egg sit where it could have a great fall?

(C2) Also, in lines 3 and 4, Humpty "couldn't be put back together." This shows he couldn't get any do-overs on his decision—not very smart!

(E) Edit reminder

Humpty Dumpty

Humpty Dumpty sat on a wall.
★ Humpty Dumpty had a great fall.
All the King's horses and all the King's men
Couldn't put Humpty Dumpty together again.

💬 **Comments**

1. I found my evidence/ details to answer the question and will put a star in the margin.
2. Now I'll put my RACE reminder in the margins of my answer.
3. I'm ready to restate the question. Restating this question without making changes would sound like this: "This decision was unwise because . . ." This sounds incomplete and doesn't flow as smoothly as I'd like. I'm going to make a few changes: "Humpty's decision to sit on the wall was unwise because . . ." sounds better.

(Available online.)

Display "Humpty Dumpty" question #2 with response (available online; see Lesson 9) on the board. Say: *When we answered question #2, we inferred that Humpty Dumpty was an egg. We also inferred that he broke into a lot of pieces when he fell. The text doesn't include either of these two details. Instead, we used our background knowledge about Humpty and about eggs to make both inferences. On the other hand, the text tells us that the King's men and horses couldn't put Humpty back together again. If we read between the lines, this suggests that Humpty Dumpty broke into many, many pieces. This confirms our thinking.*

Next, display "Little Boy Blue" (page 123) on the board, covering the question on the page. Say:

Let's look at another nursery rhyme and try to infer some things using our background knowledge and reading between the lines. We'll read this together and use text-based evidence to infer what we know about Little Boy Blue.

Read the nursery rhyme together, then ask: *What evidence do we have about Little Boy Blue's actions?*

1. We know he didn't blow his horn when he should have.
2. We know he was sleeping under a haystack when he should have been looking after the sheep.

Little Boy Blue

Little Boy Blue, come blow your horn!
The sheep's in the meadow,
The cow's in the corn.
Where is that boy who looks after the sheep?
He's under a haystack, fast asleep.

1 What does the passage tell us about Little Boy Blue? Use two details to support your answer.

(See Appendix, page 123.)

Inference: We could infer that Little Boy Blue wasn't very responsible and maybe even a little lazy. We could support this inference with the evidence in #1 and #2 above.

But this is not the only way we could answer this question. Here's another piece of evidence:

3. Based on Little Boy Blue's name, we know that he is a little or young boy.

Inference: We could infer that his chores might have been too tiring for a little boy. We could support this inference with the same evidence from #1 and #2 above.

Nailed It!

Restate and Answer With an Inference

Little Boy Blue wasn't very responsible and maybe even a little lazy.

Work Zone... Thinking in Progress

Evidence

We know he didn't blow his horn when he should have.

Evidence

We know he was sleeping under a haystack when he should have been looking after the sheep.

Nailed It!

Restate and Answer With an Inference

Little Boy Blue's chores might have been too tiring for a little boy.

Work Zone... Thinking in Progress

Evidence

We know he didn't blow his horn when he should have.

Evidence

We know he was sleeping under a haystack when he should have been looking after the sheep.

(Available online.)

In reading between and beyond the lines, we could draw these two inferences. We could use both inferences to answer the question. Both can be supported with text evidence—and in this case, even the same evidence.

To help students practice making inferences, provide them with copies of the "Nailed It!" graphic organizer (page 124), which helps them chart their thoughts and ideas on paper. Display the two completed "Nailed It!" graphic organizers (available online) on the board.

Say: *When we read between and beyond the lines in both nursery rhymes, we can make inferences about why Humpty Dumpty may have been unwise and what kind of person Little Boy Blue is. Details in the text help us form our inferences. Those details become the evidence we must include when we write our short-response answer. Using a "Nailed It!" graphic organizer also helps us think through our thoughts and ideas and make our thinking transparent. We learned how to "nail" (an idiom for "we got it!") an inference!*

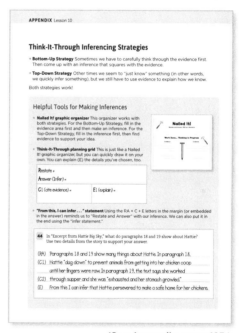

(See Appendix, page 125.)

Display "Think-It-Through Inferencing Strategies" (page 125) on the board and discuss with the class.

Close-Up #2: An Extreme Adventure

Display "An Extreme Adventure" (page 119) on the board and hand out copies. Give students a few minutes to review the article, then display question #3 (page 120) on the board and hand out copies.

(Available online.)

Say: *This question is a lot like the one about Little Boy Blue. Here, we apply our inferencing skills to a nonfiction article about swing dancer Alex Aquilino. Unlike the nursery rhyme, in which we used actions in the story to help us read between and beyond the lines for our inference, in this article, we'll use Alex's words (quotes) to read between and beyond the lines.*

Explain to students that we can also use an "infer statement" (e.g., "From this, I can infer . . .") to help us think and record—in real-time thinking— as we transfer our "in-our-head" ideas to paper. This helps us add our inference to our other important ideas. Finally, we can use a "Think-It-Through Planning Grid" (see below), which is a quick and useful way to move ideas that are inside our head to the outside. On the board, copy the planning grid below.

Sample Think-It-Through Planning Grid

Infer = Excitement outweighs stress	
C1 (paragraph 4) Performs five roles	**E (explain)** = Must know all routines
C2 (paragraph 5) Stressful but not stale	**E (explain)** = Excitement remains

Share the above sample response (available online) with students and discuss, using the comments on the page to guide your discussion. Point out the infer statement at the end of the response.

Quick Close

Say to students: *When we read between and beyond the lines of a text, we are making an inference. This deepens our understanding and "takeaways" from a passage. Inferencing also invites us to interact with a text in meaningful ways. We add our thoughts and knowledge to build our understanding. As active readers, we gain more from our reading experience.*

Independent Readiness Survey

Gauge students' comfort level with using these strategies for inferencing. Read the numbered statements below and have students respond in one of three ways:

- Thumbs up if they agree
- Thumbs down if they disagree and want more guided practice with a teacher
- Thumbs midway if they almost agree but would like to work with a partner

1. I know when I make an inference, I'm thinking beyond what's written in a text.
2. I know how to "think through" the evidence and make an inference using the strategies shared in this lesson.
3. I can independently use these strategies to help me include an inference in my short answers.

Teaching Notes

- Inferencing is a difficult skill for many students to grasp and master. The strategies in this lesson help make the thinking processes used for inferencing transparent. They also help students use text evidence to think through original ideas and claims.

- Helping students make inferences enables them to understand a text beyond a literal level. It also helps them make an evidence-based claim about the text that demonstrates their deeper-level understanding and analysis. We can help students develop skill with these complicated tasks by encouraging transparent thinking and connecting ideas.

- The "Nailed It!" graphic organizer (page 124) introduced in this lesson can help scaffold student skill with inferencing. Students can also draw a quick planning grid (modeled after the graphic organizer) to help them think through the evidence and create an inference.

- Students sometimes begin writing an answer before completely thinking it through. As a result, their response lacks a deeper-level inference. Using an "infer statement" enables them to add their good thinking to the end of their answer. As an alternative, students can draw a quick Think-It-Through Planning Grid (page 54) when they have trouble composing "in their head." They can use space anywhere on the test page (such as under the questions or passage) to help make their ideas transparent and easier to extend, shape, and refine. This planning grid is also helpful for students in Grades 4 through 8 as they must explain their answers more fully, per their grade-level standards.

- Students develop an ability to make evidence-based inferences and claims over time. Factors, such as background knowledge, often affect the rate at which this happens. In an average-size classroom, it is not unusual for teachers to find a wide range of abilities with this skill.

- Model inferential thinking by using "think-alouds." Add brief written notes to capture ideas and evidence as a way to scaffold the use of the graphic organizers in this lesson.

- Generating inferences can be thought of as a top-down or bottom-up approach. For example, skilled inference makers who automatically generate deeper interactions with the text may need to backtrack their thinking to pinpoint the evidence that led them there. These are top-down inference makers. Bottom-up inference makers must pause and study the evidence first in order to arrive at an inference.

- The distinction between valid and invalid inferences and claims depends upon the evidence provided by a student. When guiding students in response writing, encourage original, creative thinking that can be supported by the text.

- While making inferences is a challenging skill, some students are able to draw inferences and state claims easily. Likewise, they can effortlessly explain how certain evidence and details led them to their original ideas. Encourage these students to extend their skills.

LESSON 11
Strategies for Finding and Citing Evidence for Short Responses

Students investigate where to get evidence by identifying text "hot spots," how to use evidence—quotation, summary, paraphrasing, and a mixture of these—and what transition words to fluently start and connect their evidence.

Quick Start: The words *details*, *evidence*, and *support* mean the same thing. Can you think of other similar words? (*Proof, facts, data*)

Making Connections

Say to students: *Short-response questions typically ask us to "use details to support your response." This means we must prove our good ideas with facts from the text—usually two facts. We've already used some evidence skills in earlier lessons; now, we'll add muscle to them! Specifically, we'll take a close look at:*

- *WHERE we can get evidence*
- *HOW we can use evidence in our answer*
- *WHAT ways we can start to connect our evidence in our answer*

Let's begin with WHERE we get evidence.

(See Appendix, pages 126 and 127.)

Display "Where to Find Evidence in Stories & Literature" (page 126) and "Where to Find Evidence in Articles & Informational Texts" (page 127) on the board. Hand out copies to students. Say: *In stories and literature, we can find evidence from the characters, events, story plot, special ways the author writes, and more. In articles and informational texts, we can find evidence from text details, visuals and captions, key ideas, text structures and features, and techniques.*

Tell students that as they look for evidence, they can use the Find & Underline strategy—go back to the text and find and underline the evidence they can use to prove their answer. To find evidence, they should always go back to the text. Use hashtags and underlines to quickly find "hot spots" of evidence. Underline all evidence and place the related question number in the margin of the passage. If students are unsure of an answer, returning to the passage can help them think this through.

Close-Up #1: Humpty Dumpty

Display "Humpty Dumpty" question #1 with sample response (available online) on the board. Say to students: *We'll revisit our first question with Humpty Dumpty, with our hashtags and underlines in place. The question was: "What happened to Humpty Dumpty?" Let's review our answer.*

- In this simple nursery rhyme, WHERE we get the evidence is from the characters' actions and the story events.

- Next, we decide HOW we are going to include the evidence in our answer.

- In C1, we use four words from the story: he *"sat on a wall."* We didn't change the words at all. To let our reader know those are the author's words—not our words—we place them within quotation marks. This is called a *quote* or *quotation.*

- In C2, we use our own words to describe the event: *he couldn't be put back together by the King's men.* Since those are our own words, we don't need to add quotation marks. Here, we sum up (summarize) key ideas in our own words.

Humpty Dumpty

1 Humpty Dumpty sat on a wall.
2 Humpty Dumpty had a great fall. # fell
3 All the King's horses and all the King's men
4 Couldn't put Humpty Dumpty together again.
     #unable to fix

1 What happened to Humpty Dumpty?
   Use two details to support your response.

(RA) What happened to Humpty Dumpty was he broke into pieces and had a very bad day!

(C1) I know this because in lines 1 and 2, I learned he "sat on a wall" but then fell off.

(C2) Next, in lines 3 and 4, I learned he couldn't be put back together by the King's men.

(E) After writing your answer, read it over carefully for accuracy.

Comments
1. The restate and answer (RA) are shown together. I began by restating, using words from the question to start my answer. Then, I answered using my own thoughts and my own words.
2. In (C1) and (C2), I included my evidence (referred to as "details" in the question) from the text. I even added the line numbers where I found evidence in the passage. Also, I used C1 and C2 because I had to include two details to support my answer.
3. The (E) stands for Edit. This reminds me to proofread and check for accuracy.

(Available online.)

Explain to students that these are two ways we can use evidence in our answer. Display "How to Use Evidence" (page 128) on the board and discuss with the class.

Think & Discuss: How to Use Evidence

1. Use the author's words in a **quote** or **quotation**.
- Quote a complete sentence.
  "Humpty Dumpty sat on a wall."
- Quote four or five words or a phrase.
  He "sat on a wall."
- Quote one keyword.
  Humpty had a "great" fall.

How to use a quote as evidence in your answer:
- Select what and how much you want to quote. (Don't overuse the author's words and ideas. Yours are also important!)
- Copy the words just as they look in the story.
- Place quotation marks at the beginning and the end of the quote.

2. Use your own words to **sum up** (or **summarize**) main ideas or critical events.
  Humpty fell off of the wall.

3. Use your own words to **retell** (or **paraphrase**) main ideas in an article or events in a story.
  Once there was an egg named Humpty Dumpty. He climbed a wall and sat at the top. Sadly, he fell, broke, and couldn't be fixed by the King's men and horses.

How to use a summary or a retelling/paraphrase in your answer:
- Select what and how much you want to sum up or retell/paraphrase. (Don't retell details that aren't useful for your evidence.)
- Use your own words to tell the author's ideas.
- A summary tells parts of the text, and a retelling/paraphrase tells all.

(See Appendix, page 128.)

Refer back to the sample response to question #1 and say: *This example also shows WHAT words we can use to start our evidence and connect it.*

- We started C1 with the words, *"I know this because . . ."*
- We connected C1 to C2 with the word, *"Next, . . ."*
- We started C2 with the words, *"I learned . . ."*

Explain that these words are called *transitions*. They help our sentences sound clear and fluent. Display "Transition Words for Short Response" (page 128) on the board to go over other transition words students can use.

Think & Discuss: Transition Words for Short Response

Connectors (words to connect your details)	**Starters** (words to begin your details)	
• Next, . . . • Also, . . . • Additionally, . . . • Second, . . . • Furthermore, . . . • Another example . . .	• I know this because . . . • According to the text, . . . • From the reading, I know that . . . • The author says . . . • The text shows . . . • Proof of this is in . . .	• Evidence in paragraph X says . . . • As stated in paragraph X, . . . • In paragraph X, the character . . . • The author reveals/explains/expresses/shows us/notes/describes . . .

(See Appendix, page 128.)

Tell students that from the "Humpty Dumpty" question #1 sample response, we can see:

- WHERE to get evidence (where to look in a passage)
- HOW to use it (quote/quotation, sum up/summary, retell/paraphrase)
- WHAT ways we can start to connect our evidence in our answer (transition words)

Close Up #2: An Extreme Adventure

Display "An Extreme Adventure" question #1 with sample response (available online) on the board. Say: *Let's revisit our first question with "An Extreme Adventure" as well. Here, we explored a question about the main idea for a section of text.*

WHERE to locate our evidence:

- The question directs us to paragraph 6—the evidence "hot spot." After a quick review, it seems the main idea of this section is that a swing dancer is like an extreme athlete.

- Even though the evidence must come from this paragraph, it's a little challenging to pick two good details to use as evidence.

- The first detail is easy to spot. As evidence for C1, we can use the part that says the demands on a swing dancer's skills are the same as that of extreme athletes. It's right there in the paragraph.

1 What main idea is supported in paragraph 6 of "An Extreme Adventure"? Use two details to support your response.

(RA) The main idea supported in paragraph 6 of "An Extreme Adventure" is that dancing as a swing is similar to performing as an extreme athlete.

(C1) One detail that supports this is the author states the demands on Alex's "strength, agility, and stamina must parallel" the demands extreme athletes face.

(C2) Additionally, Alex has to perform five routines with "precision and artistry," which is the same expectation for extreme athletes. In sum, the main idea of paragraph 6 is that Alex must dance with the same skill as an extreme athlete performing in his or her sport.

(E) After writing your answer, read over it carefully for accuracy.

Comments
1. I restated the question then answered using my original thoughts and words.
2. I used direct quotes in C1 and C2 to strengthen my evidence.
3. I added a conclusion, which extended my answer beyond the lines provided.

(Available online.)

- For C2, we could claim that performing "with precision and artistry" is expected of an athlete as well as a swing. We're using some background knowledge here.

HOW to use the evidence:

- For C1 and C2, our answer uses a mix of quotes and our own words. This is especially helpful for the C2 evidence, which we had to construct carefully.

WHAT way to start to connect the evidence:

- We can stick to basic transition words to connect our evidence. We want to spend our time constructing our idea about expectations for C2. (Model for students that parts of a task may require different amounts of time to think through and complete.)

Tell students: *If you struggle to find evidence for your answer, consider sketching a quick planning grid* (from Lesson 10, page 54) *to help you rethink your answer. Although we knew where to get evidence in this example* (paragraph 6, as directed by the question), *we still had to explain how a detail proved our idea and worked as evidence. This took some thinking. We spent our time on this because it was important. As a result, we didn't spend as much time selecting transitions, and we stuck to the basics.*

Quick Close

Say to students: *Seeking evidence and using it correctly can be tricky. Using your close-reading and text-marking skills help. Also, learning the techniques in this Quick & Easy Lesson will help you become expert evidence hunters and users.*

Independent Readiness Survey

Gauge students' comfort level with the Cite Evidence stage of short responses. Read the numbered statements below and have students respond in one of three ways:

- Thumbs up if they agree
- Thumbs down if they disagree and want more guided practice with a teacher
- Thumbs midway if they almost agree but would like to work with a partner

1. I know how to use my hashtags (#) and underlines to find evidence "hot spots" in a passage.
2. I know how to use quotes (quotations), sum up (summarize), and/or retell (paraphrase) key evidence to include in my short response.
3. I know how to start and connect my pieces of evidence with transitions in my response.

Teaching Notes

- Students often find it challenging to select the evidence that best supports their ideas. There is a mismatch or disconnect between the two. Have students try out different transition "starters" to help them understand and clarify the connection between their ideas and the evidence.

- Younger students may have difficulty maneuvering through booklets, packets, magazines, and so on. Encourage them to use sticky notes, bookmarks, or other tools to help them build skill and comfort with finding evidence in longer reading materials.

- Helping students improve their skills with evidence is ongoing. After they master the basics, help them evaluate and choose the "strongest" piece of evidence by discussing their reasons and criteria aloud.

- Short-response questions often ask for two or three pieces of supporting evidence. Students using C1 and C2 in the RACE acronym alongside their response may also want to use check marks or numbers to recount their details. Not having enough supporting details in a response is another common error students make.

- Remind students to make use of their hashtags (#) and underlined information. Both marks should enable them to return quickly to evidence "hot spots" in a text. Help students recognize the value of their text annotations.

- Show students how to cite the location of their evidence (e.g., paragraph, stanza, or line number) after they have demonstrated an ability to locate two or three pieces of evidence. This can best be achieved during discussions and through teacher modeling. Evidence-based thinking can often support multiple answers.

- Encourage students to explore various ways they can list their evidence (e.g., direct quote, paraphrase/summary) to help improve the fluency and brevity of their response. Students may develop habits of writing too much and/or using extensive quotations or summaries. Remind them to stay focused on their RACE writing plan to help keep their responses concise and targeted.

Editing for Capitals, Understanding, Punctuation, and Spelling

Emphasize to students the importance of going back to check their answers for common errors in grammar and spelling.

Quick Start: You've written your short response. How do you make sure it says exactly what you wanted to say?

Making Connections

Tell students: *The last step in our RACE writing process is editing. Some think this is the most important stage. Why? This step helps ensure your whole answer—from start to finish—looks exactly the way you like it. It's a grand finale! This can be quite challenging.*

There's a simple process we can follow to make editing easier: The Proofread to Perfection process! It helps you take charge of the editing process, guides you through key steps, and reminds you to use everything you've learned. What are some things to check for? Let's take a close look!

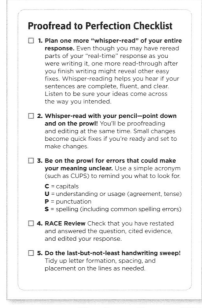

Proofread to Perfection Checklist

☐ **1. Plan one more "whisper-read" of your entire response.** Even though you may have reread parts of your "real-time" response as you were writing it, one more read-through after you finish writing might reveal other easy fixes. Whisper-reading helps you hear if your sentences are complete, fluent, and clear. Listen to be sure your ideas come across the way you intended.

☐ **2. Whisper-read with your pencil—point down and on the prowl!** You'll be proofreading and editing at the same time. Small changes become quick fixes if you're ready and set to make changes.

☐ **3. Be on the prowl for errors that could make your meaning unclear.** Use a simple acronym (such as CUPS) to remind you what to look for.
   C = capitals
   U = understanding or usage (agreement, tense)
   P = punctuation
   S = spelling (including common spelling errors)

☐ **4. RACE Review** Check that you have restated and answered the question, cited evidence, and edited your response.

☐ **5. Do the last-but-not-least handwriting sweep!** Tidy up letter formation, spacing, and placement on the lines as needed.

(See Appendix, page 129.)

CUPS Checklist

☐ **Capitals**
   Check for capitals at the beginning of a sentence, proper nouns, MINTS (months, the letter *I*, names, titles, start of sentences)

☐ **Understanding**
   Whisper-read sentences to helps you listen to your ideas and check for:
   • agreement
   • tense
   • pronoun
   • a clumsy-sounding sentence for a variety of reasons

☐ **Punctuation**
   • punctuation at the end of sentences
   • correct use of commas

☐ **Spelling**

(See Appendix, page 129.)

Display the "Proofread to Perfection Checklist" (page 129) on the board and hand out copies. You may also want to distribute and discuss the "CUPS Checklist" (page 129).

Remind students that editing real-time writing is very different from editing traditional writing-process pieces. They can't get help from classmates or teachers, as they might in "peer edit" or "teacher check" processes. Also, they won't have access to resources, such as word walls, dictionaries, or spell checks. Instead, students will have to edit on their own.

Close-Up #1: Humpty Dumpty

Display "Humpty Dumpty" question #2 with proofreading marks (available online) on the board. Say to students: *This example shows typical corrections to real-time writing corrections. When we whisper-read, we can see some easy fixes. For example, we forgot to include the word* not *in the first sentence. This easy fix helped our words match our ideas! Also, our answer rambled with a lot of "ands" connecting ideas. To fix this, we gave each idea its own sentence. Our "CUPS Checklist" helped us find other errors.*

2 At the beginning of the nursery rhyme, Humpty Dumpty decides to sit on a wall. Why was this decision unwise? Use two details from the story to support your answer.

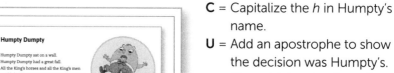

Humpty Dumpty

Humpty Dumpty sat on a wall.
Humpty Dumpty had a great fall.
All the King's horses and all the King's men
Couldn't put Humpty Dumpty together again.

CUPS

(RA) humpty's decision to sit on the wall was unwise because it was **not** a safe place for him to be.

(C1) I know this because in line 2, he had a "great fall" off the wall, which tells me he didn't think this ~~threw~~ **through** very carefully. and why would an egg sit where it could have a "great fall"?

(C2) ~~And~~ **Also** in line**s** 3 and 4, Humpty "couldn't be put back together." This shows he broke into **#** alot of pieces. He didn't get any do-overs on his decision — not very smart.

(E)

(Available online.)

C = Capitalize the *h* in Humpty's name.

U = Add an apostrophe to show the decision was Humpty's. Also add the plural *s* to *line* as we meant two lines (3 and 4).

P = Add a period after *pieces*.

S = Fix the spelling of *alot* by adding space to show two words. Also fix spelling of *through* instead of the homophone *threw*.

Tell students to also review their RACE reminders and check off each one to be sure their answer includes everything.

Close-Up #2: An Extreme Adventure

Display "An Extreme Adventure" question #2 with proofreading marks (available online) on the board. Tell students: *This response shows other, less typical but important corrections to short responses. When we whisper-read, we may realize that our details and explanation need some light revisions. So we could add more details at the bottom of our answer and draw insert arrows to show where these new details belong. We can also make CUPS revisions to other sentences so the whole answer sounds more fluent.*

2 Why is paragraph 1 of "An Extreme Adventure" an effective introduction? Use two details to support your answer.

Paragraph 1 of "An Extreme Adventure" is an effective introduction because the reader is immediately hooked and wonders what the next new extreme event could be. For example, the reader wants to read on to find out what **sport is** is next. Additionally, the reader thinks about the kind of information the author is likely to include. Achieving all of these goals at the same time makes an **e**ffective introduction.

is introduced to the topic of extreme sports through the author's list, which includes bungee jumping, snowboarding, and zip lining, and

is excited to use the clues "dizzying speeds, grueling demands, and DANGER" (in capital letters) to

(Available online.)

C = n/a

U = Add "sport is" after *what's* (while also deleting the apostrophe *s*) to clarify. Also, delete *s* in *thinks* to reflect correct grammatical construction of the new sentence.

P = n/a

S = Fix the spelling of the word *effective* by changing the *a* to an *e*.

Say: *Even though we had previously checked all of the RACE components, our response is much stronger now that we've revised it by adding more details and explanations.*

Quick Close

Explain to students that these simple take-charge editing strategies and the editing process help make sure that their short answers make their good ideas shine in every way.

Independent Readiness Survey

Gauge students' comfort level with using the editing strategies in their short responses. Read the numbered statements below and have students respond in one of three ways:

- Thumbs up if they agree
- Thumbs down if they disagree and want more guided practice with a teacher
- Thumbs midway if they almost agree but would like to work with a partner

1. I understand that the Proofread to Perfection Checklist is a final check that helps me take charge of my own editing.
2. I know how to use CUPS (or another proofreading strategy) to make quick edits.
3. I can independently use both strategies together to help me write clear and concise answers.

Teaching Notes

- You can build differentiated "look-outs" into the editing process. "Look-outs" are specific alerts to editing errors a student may regularly make, such as not capitalizing characters' names, using too many "ands" in a response, and so on.

- Some students may wish to jot down the CUPS acronym near their response-writing area as a reminder of what to look for when proofreading.

- Integrate routine editing methods into students' real-time writing practices to help them adapt and apply these important skills.

- Have students practice the Proofread to Perfection process often to help them notice errors that might otherwise go undetected. Sometimes students "adjust" errors as they read.

CHAPTER 3

Quick & Easy Strategies for Writing Extended Responses

Do your students have a plan to write an effective extended response? Most students feel a mild sense of uneasiness when faced with an extended-response question. Questions can be lengthy and sometimes look complex with a mix of sentences, bullets, and boldface words. Most also require students to include details from two separate passages. Clearly, these tasks require a depth and scope of thinking that can intimidate even the most enthusiastic test-taker (and we've all had a few of these near-unstoppable marvels)! Adding to this, the two or three blank pages or amount of space provided for a response can feel overwhelming. Thank goodness we can help build students' confidence and ease their minds by providing a plan of action!

Buzz & Chatter

Common Nationwide Practices

Methods of evaluating student skill with lengthier responses on standardized tests vary from state to state. Still, there are some shared characteristics that stand out. For example, extended-response questions are, for the most part, more demanding compared to the short-response questions. Most contain multiple ideas and therefore require a lengthier, multiple-paragraph answer. Additionally, students are gently urged to plan their extended response prior to writing, even though their plan is not graded. Ample planning space for this optional-but-encouraged prewriting activity is often provided. Finally, students are reminded to edit and, at times, even revise their work. Clearly, a common nationwide practice is for students to adapt some form of writing process—plan, draft, edit, and revise—during these real-time writing tasks.

Adapting and Adding to the Quick & Easy Strategies

The good news is that students can apply all of the short-response strategies they've learned in Chapter 2 to their extended responses. For example, they can call upon the RACE strategy as a real-time writing process, as well as the Question-Attack, finding evidence, and editing strategies. This chapter provides quick and easy ways to amp up, adapt, and target all of these strategies to meet the formidable demands of extended-response questions and lead students toward bold, new directions.

Transparent Planning With the RACE Strategy

It is crucial for students to master simple ways to plan an extended response. We have all read responses that contain underdeveloped and fragmented ideas. These "disorganized brain dumps" (as one of my good-natured colleagues humorously calls them) are often a telltale sign that a student had no plan. Encouraging young thinker-writers to bring their planning out into the open—to make it transparent—will likely help them all. Even strong thinker-writers will reap benefits from some amount of external planning.

A transparent plan:

- **makes ideas concrete.** When students' ideas have visible shape and substance, they become easier to define, refine, and polish.
- **encourages strategic thinking.** Students can assign value, weight, and position to details and integrate them with targeted intent into a response. They can juggle parts into what will become a well-shaped whole.
- **tracks progress.** Students can evaluate the content quality of their entire response before writing it and take action to strengthen or adjust their plan as needed.

Although students won't likely have the time (or stamina) to plan in the same way they would a traditional writing-process piece, they'll still benefit from some method of planning. Happily, there are ways to improvise and use several quick and easy shortcuts to craft a real-time writing plan. Some of the shortcut strategies featured in this chapter include:

- flash formatting – quickly setting up a planning grid or organizer
- coding – adopting a "keep it thrifty" attitude by using abbreviations and brief notes
- quick timing – holding spots for items that will be written into the essay in real time, such as transition words/phrases, an introduction, and a conclusion

Introducing the RACE Real-Time Planner

A "RACE Real-Time Planner" is a blown-up and stacked version of the RACE paragraph plan used for short responses (Chapter 2). In this planner, multiple RACE "clusters" are stacked together and the *E* (for edit) is moved to the end. Students can simply draw a quick grid or modified T-square and jot the letters into place. They "flash format" their planning area with this briskly created chart. (See page 130 for a full-page version.)

RACE Real-Time Planner

FIGURE 8

I (introduction)[1]	
RA #1 (restate/answer)	C1 (cite evidence)
	C2
RA #2	C1
	C2
RA #3	C1
	C2
C (conclusion)[2]	
E (edit)	

[1] The *I* serves as a placeholder/reminder for an introduction. It will be written using words from the task.
[2] The *C* serves as a placeholder/reminder for a conclusion. It will be based on the introduction.

Just as with short responses, the *RACE* letters remind students what they need to include: Restate, Answer/infer, Cite evidence, and Edit. The RACE Real-Time Planner is a flexible checklist and organizer to help guide student thinking and written responses. The number of clusters (RA and C) depends upon the task.

Note: As discussed in Chapter 2, there are other acronyms that can serve as helpful reminders to our thinker-writers. Likewise, there are other ways to shape the RACE acronym so it is grade-level appropriate; for example, RADDE or ACED.

Must-Haves for Extended Responses

The RACE Real-Time Planner addresses the components found on most state extended-response rubrics. In the planner, each paragraph—or RACE cluster—is evaluated for alignment to expectations, just as the whole response must also meet expectations.

FIGURE 9

Must-Haves to Include in an Extended Response (as per most standards-based rubrics)	RACE Planner
Organization, coherence	**R** = restate
Purpose, audience	**A** = answer
Evidence/elaboration	**C** = cite evidence
Conventions	**E** = edit

Extended-Response Question Format — A Nationwide Practice

The format of extended-response questions varies from state to state. For example, some states frame a question within the context of a classroom event, and students write a multi-paragraph opinion/argument or informational essay in response (a narrative mode may also be used). Other states' assessments ground the question in reading passages, and students write an informational essay reflecting their insights about the passages. Still others fall somewhere in between and extend the question beyond the context of the reading passages, yet not too far.

In all cases, students must:

- understand and analyze the reading passages carefully
- grasp the purpose of (and audience for) their written task
- command use of the ideas found in their reading within their writing

The quick and easy strategies shared in this chapter are useful for all question formats.

Adding Variety to Your Lesson Instruction

When teaching extended-response writing, consider using a variety of approaches. Otherwise, the lesson could be long, boring, and consume too much of your instructional time.

In addition to showing students the completed sample responses from the lesson Close-Ups, you might also share exemplars from past tests (most states make them available). Have students guess the grade a sample paper received on a state rubric to add novelty to your lessons.

You might also choose to "tell and discuss" rather than practice some extended-response writing. For example, you might have students practice drawing and completing several RACE Real-Time Planners to improve their speed and skill in making notes. However, they don't need to write all of the essays they plan. This could be counterproductive. Instead, carefully select which essays you want students to write or which parts of an essay you want them to practice, such as the introduction or one or two RACE clusters (body paragraphs).

Practicing with puzzle essays is another way to mix up lessons. Here, students complete a partially written essay as they learn how to structure and organize an essay, add evidence, or prepare an introduction or conclusion. There are many ways you can use puzzle essays.

Finally, if your objective is to have students practice writing extended responses, you might wish to use passages you have already read. Reading and text-marking new passages every time you want to practice writing may be time prohibitive. Likewise, students remember high-interest, well-written passages. You can use and reuse these passages for several different kinds of writing activities.

Computer-Based Testing and Extended-Response Questions

While most computer-based testing (CBT) platforms offer ample blank space for extended-response questions, the ways in which they encourage planning the response differs.

Some states that use CBT distribute a blank sheet of scratch paper to students. Students plan their response on the paper (which is controlled and turned in with tests) and then compose their essays electronically on their designated device. Some districts instruct students to plan and write their essay on the scratch paper and then type the essay, with minor revisions and edits, on their devices. This seems to be a temporary fix, done largely to compensate for students' growing yet slow, choppy keyboarding skills. Shaping original ideas into fluent sentences while simultaneously hunting for correct keys on a keyboard can be tiresome and draining.

Helping students develop keyboarding fluency is on many districts' must-do lists!

Some districts also use the notes function, which is available on most CBT platforms. Students can devise a form of graphic organizer to which they can easily add notes, symbols, and segments of cut-and-pasted text.

Moving students toward flexible planning and away from reliance on a rigid, physical graphic organizer seems the best way to prepare them for future success. When students have an informed understanding (learned and practiced) of a graphic organizer, such as the RACE Real-Time Planner, and how it functions to organize and order their ideas, they can move its image into working memory and remold its shape as needed—such as by adapting it to a notes function. Creative problem solving and improvising, like this, is fast becoming the new norm.

Applying the RACE Strategy to Extended-Response Writing

LESSON 13

Introduce students to the RACE Real-Time Planner and the many ways they can use it to help guide their thinking and flexibly organize their extended writing.

Quick Start: Do you have a plan for writing an extended response?

Making Connections

Tell students: *You've read a few passages carefully, and you've answered some short-response questions. You've used close reading and RACE strategies. Now, you must answer an extended-response question. What's your plan? Wouldn't it be great if a plan that used the RACE approach worked for extended responses, too? Good news—it does! Let's take a close look.*

Display the "RACE Real-Time Planner" (page 130) on the board. Point out where each of the letters in RACE go in the planner.

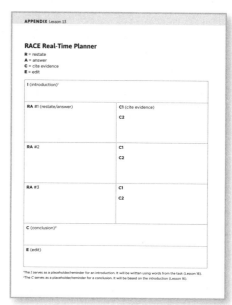

(See Appendix, page 130.)

Close-Up #1: Humpty Dumpty & Little Boy Blue

Say to students: *Let's begin with two easy-to-read nursery rhymes, "Humpty Dumpty" and "Little Boy Blue." We'll use a RACE Real-Time Planner to help us answer an extended-response question about these passages. We'll use our text-marked passages and see how to plan and write our response. The question asks:* What is a lesson that "Humpty Dumpty" and "Little Boy Blue" teach children?

Display the nursery rhymes on the board to review them. Then display question #31 (page 131) on the board and hand out copies. Read the question aloud. Say: *The bullets in the question are the main tasks. We'll give each main task its own RACE cluster. The first two bullets list what we need to answer, while the third is simply a reminder to use both texts. So we'll stack two RACE clusters in our planner. Let's "flash format" our planner, draw a grid, and leave blanks to fill in after we've given the tasks some thought.*

On the board, sketch a planner with two stacked clusters (see right). Say: *We'll "quick-time" our introduction and conclusion by writing* I *at the top and* C *at the bottom to hold spots for them.* Have students do the same on their copy.

Ask: *What are some lessons in these stories? Let's use the RACE planner to help us make inferences.* Discuss the text-marked passages and encourage students to "dig deep" and find a common theme between the two stories.

Allow time for students to fill in their planner, saying: *Get on your thrifty attitude and code your responses. Use keywords and ideas, not complete sentences, and abbreviate the characters' names to keep your notes short. We'll practice other ways to shorten our note-taking over time. We don't want a lengthy plan that we just rewrite when it's time to write our response. That wouldn't make sense.*

If you want to, share the sample RACE Real-Time Planner (available online) with students and discuss as a class.

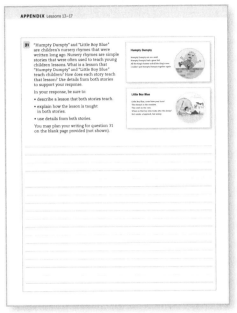

(See Appendix, page 131.)

RACE Real-Time Planner

I (introduction)

RA #1 (restate/answer)	**C1** (cite evidence) **C2**
RA #2	**C1** **C2**

C (conclusion)

E (edit)

I = (titles, genres, authors + key ideas from task paraphrased in own words)	
(RA1) A lesson both teach is ... make smart choices.	**(C1)** HD = makes foolish choice to sit on wall **(C2)** LBB = chooses to sleep instead of work
(RA2) The lesson is taught when ... their unwise choices backfire.	**(C1)** HD makes a foolish choice, sits on wall, falls, & can't be put back together **(C2)** LBB isn't at job, is asleep instead, cows & sheep wander away, people look for him

C = (circle back to intro with theme added)

E = (edit reminder)

(Available online.)

Close-Up #2: When Looks Matter & It Came From the Mud

Say: *Let's try another question using the paired passages "When Looks Matter" (which we've read and marked up in earlier lessons) and "It Came From the Mud" (which is new). Let's start by close-reading and text-marking this second passage.*

(See Appendix, pages 132 and 133.)

Hand out copies of "It Came From the Mud" (page 132) and give students time to close-read and text-mark the passage. Afterward, display question #32 (page 133) on the board and hand out copies.

Say to students: *This question is about how some animals use their special features to help them survive. In this format, the tasks are given within the question, while the bullets remind us that we need an introduction and conclusion and that we must use information from both passages. It also reminds us that our essay should have multiple paragraphs.*

Explain that to flash format their RACE Real-Time Planner, they want to make sure they know what the question is asking for—an essay that explains the features some fish and mammals have that help them survive. Have students scan the two articles and look over their underlines and hashtags. They want to find two or three examples they can use in their essay. Say: *We can use the pangolin from the first passage and the mudskipper and seahorse from passage 2. Let's stack three RACE clusters for our essay, one for each animal.*

Draw a quick RACE Real-Time Planner with three clusters stacked on the board (see below). Then say: *Next, we'll jot brief notes that we can shape into sentences when we write. We should probably note which passage the information came from using P1 or P2. This will help make sure we use both passages—and remind us which passage to return to if needed.*

Have students draw their own planner and scan the passages to help them fill out their planner. Afterward, share the sample planner (available online) with students and discuss.

I = (titles, genres, authors + key ideas from task paraphrased in own words)	
(RA1) first is the pangolin (P1) covered in scales	**(C1)** covered from head to tail **(C2)** body armor protects from predators, like tigers with teeth
(RA2) second is the mudskipper (P2) body parts help it survive in water & land	**(C1)** fins & tails for movement **(C2)** gills to breathe
(RA3) third is seahorse (P2) strange body parts help it get food	**(C1)** snouts suck up shrimp **(C2)** tail can grab plants

C = (circle back to intro with main idea added)

E = (edit reminder)

(Available online.)

Quick Close

Tell students: *The RACE Real-Time Planner strategy is useful for writing extended responses. With this strategy, we group and stack RACE clusters based on the task. Each RACE cluster reminds us about what to include and how to organize our ideas. It works well with a lot of different kinds of questions and passages. Finally, it works hand-in-hand with close-reading and text-marking strategies.*

Independent Readiness Survey

Gauge students' comfort level with using the RACE Real-Time Planner for extended responses. Read the numbered statements below and have students respond in one of three ways:

- Thumbs up if they agree
- Thumbs down if they disagree and want more guided practice with a teacher
- Thumbs midway if they almost agree but would like to work with a partner

1. I know the RACE Real-Time Planner helps remind me what to include and how to organize my ideas.
2. I know how to quickly draw a RACE Real-Time Planner.
3. I can independently use the RACE Real-Time Planner to plan a well-developed response.

Teaching Notes

- Remind students of the differences between an extended response and a short response. While the RACE acronym is helpful for both, the expectations for an extended response are greater than those for a short response, based on state assessment rubrics and many districts' rubrics. Share your state rubric (or a student-friendly version) with your class so they know what's expected of them.

- To flash format a RACE Real-Time Planner, encourage students to use their Question-Attack skills (covered in-depth in Lesson 14) and their knowledge of structuring a strong response.

- Students often overwrite in their planner until they gain experience working with thrifty notes. Writing confidently from fewer notes is a learning process that takes place over time.

- Remind students that in a test, short-response questions sometimes contain helpful information they can use in an extended-response question, which typically follows.

- Extended-response questions often ask students to write about and explain their understanding of whole passages or a single passage (if paired passages are not used). Identifying and comparing themes or main ideas are common. This can be tricky for some students. Ongoing classroom instruction with these literary basics is always helpful.

- To show their understanding of a passage, students may be asked to explain, describe, or discuss elements of the text or to apply their understanding to a related task. Practice the format used in your state assessments to help students gain confidence and apply these strategies effectively.

- As you continue to practice with the RACE Real-Time Planner, you may wish to work with short passages or ones you've already read and text-marked as a class to limit demands on student stamina and on your instructional time.

- During extended-response instruction and practice, use a combination of show, tell, write, and remember. Mix up your teaching methods to help keep lessons moving. Use passages you've already read, show completed examples, or discuss how a challenging matter could be solved. While it is also important to keep up the routine—model, scaffold, independent application, and continuous teacher monitoring—isolating and targeting skills during instruction may be helpful and time-saving.

- The amount of space provided on a state assessment is a helpful indicator of the amount of writing that is expected. For extended responses, students should thoroughly develop their good ideas, which takes time and space. Students may need to rely more on their planner if their ideas continue to be underdeveloped.

- Remind students that the RACE Real-Time Planner is flexible—there is no single right answer. Evidence-based thinking can often support multiple answers. Build student skill and confidence during discussions and through teacher modeling.

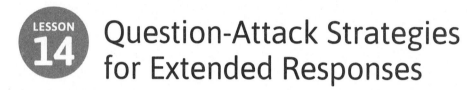

LESSON 14 Question-Attack Strategies for Extended Responses

Show students how to "flash format" their RACE Real-Time Planners based on the format of the question.

Quick Start: What Question-Attack strategies work best for extended-response questions?

Making Connections

Tell students: *You've answered short-response questions using Question-Attack strategies (Lesson 9). Will these strategies work for extended-response questions, too? They will! Let's take a close look at the ones that work best and the ones that we can easily tweak or adapt to help us answer different kinds of extended-response questions.*

Note: You may wish to review the Question-Attack strategies featured in Lesson 9.

Close-Up #1: Humpty Dumpty & Little Boy Blue

Explain to students that the Question-Attack strategies help us in two ways:

1. They help us understand the task by looking closely at each question we must answer.

2. They help us use our restating skills to set up our RACE Real-Time Planner and guide our thinking.

Say: *Let's see this in action using the two easy-to-read nursery rhymes and the question about a lesson children learn in them.*

Display "Humpty Dumpty" and "Little Boy Blue" on the board to review them, then display question #31 (page 131). Read the question aloud.

Remind students that Question-Attack strategies help us close-read a question so we understand what the question is asking. This is true for short- and extended-response questions. In this extended-response task, the questions are repeated in separate bullets below the task. Show students how easy it is to text-mark the questions in both areas using the strategies they learned from Lesson 9. Model text-marking the task as you think aloud (see question #31 on next page).

31 "Humpty Dumpty" and "Little Boy Blue" are children's nursery rhymes that were written long ago. Nursery rhymes are simple stories that were often used to teach young children lessons. What is a lesson that "Humpty Dumpty" and "Little Boy Blue" teach children? How does each story teach that lesson? Use details from both stories to support your response.

In your response, be sure to:
- describe a lesson that both stories teach.
- explain how the lesson is taught in both stories.
- use details from both stories.

You may plan your writing for question 31 on the blank page provided (not shown).

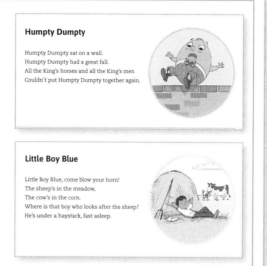

Humpty Dumpty

Humpty Dumpty sat on a wall.
Humpty Dumpty had a great fall.
All the King's horses and all the King's men
Couldn't put Humpty Dumpty together again.

Little Boy Blue

Little Boy Blue, come blow your horn!
The sheep's in the meadow,
The cow's in the corn.
Where is that boy who looks after the sheep?
He's under a haystack, fast asleep.

(Available online.)

- In lengthy questions, circle the question mark and work backward to find the question.
- Box the clue words (*what* and *how*) in the question.
- Review students' understanding of instruction words, such as *describe* or *explain*.

Say: *After marking the question, we can be confident that we know what this task is asking us to do. There are two tasks we must address: describe a lesson and explain how it is taught in both rhymes.*

Another component of the Question-Attack strategies is restating the question. (You may wish to review the Restating the Question Checklist on page 122 as well.) Tell students: *Remember that restating the question helps us get started when we answer a short-response question. The same is true for extended-response questions.* Restating *means to use some of the words from the question in our answer.* Invite students to suggest ways to restate the questions from the task.

Close-Up #2: When Looks Matter & It Came From the Mud

Invite students to look at another question using the paired nonfiction passages "When Looks Matter" and "It Came From the Mud." Display question #32 (page 133) on the board and hand out copies to students. Say: *For these informational articles, the process of using Question-Attack strategies is the same. We'll use our close-reading and text-marking skills to be sure we understand the task and answer all questions.* Model underlining keywords for the task as you think aloud (see question #32 on next page).

- This task is asking us to explain the features that some fish and mammals have that help them survive.

- This will be an informational essay, so it makes sense that we must include an introduction and a conclusion.

- The question we'll restate and use to flash format our RACE Real-Time Planner is: *What are some features that help fish and mammals survive?* We'll try to locate three examples from the articles and stack them in our planner. Then we'll think about how to restate the question for each example.

32 Scientists who study <u>fish and mammals</u> explain that they look the way they do often because their <u>survival depends on it</u>. In other words, these creatures may have special, easy-to-see features that help them survive in their environments. Write an <u>essay</u> that <u>explains</u> the <u>features</u> that <u>some fish and mammals have</u> that help them <u>survive</u>. Be sure to use facts and details from both passages to support your explanation.

Be sure to include:

- an <u>introduction</u>
- <u>support</u> for your ideas using information from the passages
- a <u>conclusion</u> that is relevant

Your response should be in the form of a <u>multiple-paragraph essay</u>. You may plan your writing for question 32 on the blank page provided (not shown).

(Available online.)

Quick Close

Tell students that Question-Attack and restating strategies help us understand and answer all parts of an extended-response task. They are helpful for planning a lot of different kinds of extended-writing tasks—from narrative stories to informational essays. It's easy to adapt them. They also work with different kinds of passages—single, paired, fiction, nonfiction. Finally, they make use of our close-reading and Text-Marking strategies in unique ways. Finding new ways to apply things we already know helps us grow as independent learners.

Independent Readiness Survey

Gauge students' comfort level with using the Question-Attack strategies for extended-response tasks. Read the numbered statements below and have students respond in one of three ways:

- Thumbs up if they agree
- Thumbs down if they disagree and want more guided practice with a teacher
- Thumbs midway if they almost agree but would like to work with a partner

1. I know how to mark extended-response questions using the Question-Attack strategies.
2. I know how to restate questions (and make changes, if necessary) to help plan my extended-response answers.
3. I can independently use both strategies together to help me write clear, concise, and complete answers.

Teaching Notes

- The Question-Attack strategies help students break down tasks and isolate questions. As extended-response tasks are often longer and more complex than short-response questions, these strategies help build student understanding as well as confidence.
- The strategies can be applied to many different types of questions and can therefore help students at any grade level, with any subject area, and both inside and outside of school.
- With practice, students will bring their own unique coding style to the Question-Attack strategies. Some will continue to circle, box, and underline words, while others will simply

underline or even highlight, especially once they work exclusively on electronic devices. As there is no single "right way" to apply the strategies, encourage students to mark the questions in a manner that makes sense to them.

- Invite students to share and discuss with classmates how they applied the Question-Attack strategies to a complex question.

- As students practice their Question-Attack strategies, make sure they are familiar with words and phrases that may be tricky or unfamiliar. (Photocopy and distribute the "Tricky Words/Phrases" chart on page 134 as needed).

- Using colored highlighters to isolate the question words (*who, what, when, where, why,* and *how*) and/or the question mark is another way to help ensure students understand the task and answer it thoroughly.

- Questions that include words such as *explain, describe,* or *discuss* will take more practice to answer effectively than the typical 5W questions. Ongoing modeling and practice will improve student understanding.

- Have students check or cross off tasks as they complete each one (or transfer them to their

(See Appendix, page 134.)

RACE Real-Time Planner) or write the number of questions that appear in a task. This provides a check system that ensures their response is complete.

Wielding Evidence for Extended Responses
LESSON 15

Students learn how to evaluate the strength or weight of their evidence and how to determine where to place their evidence.

Quick Start: What evidence-wielding strategies work best for extended-response questions?

Making Connections

Tell students: *You've answered short-response questions using your evidence-seeking skills (Lesson 11). Can we use these strategies for extended-response questions, too? Yes! Let's take a close look at those that work best and those that we can easily tweak or adapt to help us with different kinds of extended-response questions. In this lesson, we'll learn how to build our evidence-seeking strategies within our RACE Real-Time Planner.*

You may wish to review the "Where to Find Evidence" handouts from Lesson 11 (pages 126 and 127).

Close-Up #1: Humpty Dumpty & Little Boy Blue

Display question #31 (page 131) on the board and hand out copies. Remind students that this task includes questions about two reading passages. These kinds of tasks ask us to demonstrate our ability to read, think, and write from two sources. Review what students have learned in Lesson 11:

- WHERE to locate evidence (fiction and nonfiction)
- HOW to use evidence (quote, summarize, paraphrase)
- WHAT transition words to use to connect evidence (*also*, *additionally*, and so on)

Tell students that they'll make good use of these strategies and build even more as they tackle extended-response tasks. In this lesson, they'll learn how to plan their use of evidence in their RACE Real-Time Planner. Specifically, they'll learn how to:

- balance evidence with their original thinking
- weigh evidence and select the strongest
- evenly spread the evidence so all questions in the task have strong, developed answers

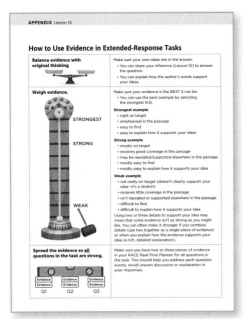

(See Appendix, page 135.)

Display "How to Use Evidence in Extended-Response Tasks" (page 135) on the board and discuss with students.

Say to students: *Be sure to prepare your RACE Real-Time Planner in a way that shows your skills in reading and writing from two sources.* Set up a RACE planner on the board like the one shown below, thinking aloud as you fill it in. Have students follow along on their copies.

- First, we'll set up a planner using the questions in the task. We'll leave the answers blank for now and hold a place for the introduction with an *I* and the conclusion with a *C*.

- Next, we'll go back to the nursery rhymes and hunt for clues about the first question: *Describe a lesson both stories teach.* Let's review our text-marking.

- Neither text states exactly what lesson was taught, but it seems both characters had problems because they didn't make smart choices. So, a lesson the stories teach is that it's important to make smart choices.

- For evidence, we can say that the lesson is taught because each character made a foolish choice that turned out badly. Use abbreviations for the titles and in other places to save time.

- Now, let's go to the RACE Real-Time Planner and add that the lesson both stories teach is to make smart choices (RA1). This is original thinking, which we want to balance with the

I = (titles, genres, authors + key ideas from task paraphrased in own words)	
(RA1) A lesson both teach is … make smart choices.	**(C1)** HD = makes foolish choice to sit on wall **(C2)** LBB = chooses to sleep instead of work
(RA2) The lesson is taught when … their unwise choices backfire.	**(C1)** HD makes a foolish choice, sits on wall, falls, & can't be put back together **(C2)** LBB isn't at job, is asleep instead, cows & sheep wander away, people look for him

C = (circle back to intro with theme added)
E = (edit reminder)

(Available online.)

evidence we use from the passage. We can also add the evidence that both characters made foolish choices—Humpty Dumpty by sitting on a wall (C1) and Little Boy Blue by sleeping instead of doing his work (C2).

- Repeat this process for the next question in the RACE Real-Time Planner: *How does each story teach that lesson?* Let's review our text-marking again.

- For RA2, we can answer that their unwise choices backfired. For evidence, we can explain more about the characters' foolish choices and how each one led to problems. Use key details from each rhyme and put a star by the evidence we plan to use in the answer.
  - HD sits on wall, falls, and can't be put back together (C1)
  - LBB isn't at his job, is asleep instead, cows & sheep wander away, and people are looking for him (C2)

Check over the RACE Real-Time Planner to make sure all questions are restated and include a straightforward answer. Each has cited evidence to prove the answers.

Tell students: *From Close-Up #1, we can see that:*

- *planning what evidence to use and how we will use it to support our ideas is simplified when we use our RACE Real-Time Planner.*

- *we can set up our planner quickly and easily and take our time to go back to the text to think through the best way to answer the questions. We can also build and explain our support for our ideas with strong text-based evidence.*

Close-Up #2: When Looks Matter & It Came From the Mud

Display question #32 (page 133) on the board and hand out copies. Say to students: *Let's try another example.*

Set up a planner on the board like the one shown below, thinking aloud as you fill it in.

- First, we'll set up a planner in a way that makes sense. Like in our earlier one, we'll hold a place for the introduction with an *I* and the conclusion with a *C*. Now, let's go back to both articles to identify fish and mammals that use special features to survive. We can use our text-marking to find "evidence hot spots."

- "When Looks Matter" includes facts about the blobfish, proboscis monkey, frog, and pangolin. But the strongest example is the pangolin—details are right on target, emphasized in the passage, and easy to find.

I = (titles, genres, authors + key ideas from task paraphrased in own words)

(RA1) first is the pangolin (P1) covered in scales	**(C1)** covered from head to tail **(C2)** body armor protects from predators, like tigers with teeth
(RA2) second is the mudskipper (P2) body parts help it survive in water & land	**(C1)** fins & tails for movement **(C2)** gills to breathe
(RA3) third is seahorse (P2) strange body parts help it get food	**(C1)** snouts suck up shrimp **(C2)** tail can grab plants

C = (circle back to intro with main idea added)

E = (edit reminder)

(Available online.)

- "It Came From the Mud" includes facts about the mudskipper, seahorse, flying fish, and archerfish. The strongest example is the mudskipper—details are right on target and the animal is featured in the passage.
- We should include one more example to make sure our essay is strong. The article has two solid details about the seahorse that will balance well with the other examples we've selected.
- Now that we have good examples with strong and evenly balanced evidence, we can add notes in the RACE Real-Time Planner.

Have students fill out their own RACE Real-Time Planner to respond to the question. Tell them they can abbreviate titles as P1 for the first passage and P2 for the second one. When they're done, remind them to check over their planner to make sure they have restated all questions and included a straightforward answer for each one. Be sure each has cited evidence to prove their answers.

After students have completed their own planner, say: *From Close Up #2, we can see:*

- *the process of adding ideas to our RACE Real-Time Planner when we respond to different types of tasks is also simple.*
- *wielding our evidence is similar for different types of tasks.*

Quick Close

Say to students: *We've added to our skills, and now we know how to make the best use of evidence. We know how to balance it with our own original thinking. We know how to judge the weight of the evidence and select it carefully based on its strength. We also know how to make sure all parts of our response are solid so the whole thing holds together firmly.*

Independent Readiness Survey

Gauge students' comfort level with wielding evidence in their extended responses. Read the numbered statements below and have students respond in one of three ways:

- Thumbs up if they agree
- Thumbs down if they disagree and want more guided practice with a teacher
- Thumbs midway if they almost agree but would like to work with a partner

1. I know how to use my own ideas together with evidence I find in a passage in my extended responses.
2. I know how to weigh and balance evidence to use in my extended response.
3. I can independently cite evidence (C1 & C2) in my RACE Real-Time Planner.

Teaching Notes

- Students can set up the format for their RACE Real-Time Planner at any time. They can add RACE clusters based on the number of questions in the task. Each cluster will restate and answer the question (RA) and include cited evidence (C1 and C2) with some explanation. (For upper-grade planners, you may want to have them use E1 and E2 to show explanations.)
- With practice, students learn to code their evidence into their RACE Real-Time Planner (the code corresponds to specific parts of the passage) or abbreviate their ideas more efficiently. Students should take roughly 7 to 10 minutes to complete their RACE Real-Time Planners.
- Teach students how to evaluate the strength or weight of their evidence. For example, recognizing which detail is strong, stronger, or strongest in terms of supporting a point in an argument is a factor they will want to consider.

- Students should also explore how to gauge where to place their evidence: Does it support their first point or their second point best? Most extended-response questions contain multiple ideas, so determining how best to puzzle in the details may take some jockeying.

- Students often need practice to recognize how to *align* evidence to their ideas. Juggling evidence and determining where it fits best is a skill they can practice in ELA and content-area instruction.

- In complex tasks with multiple passages and multiple questions, students may struggle to find enough support or strong support. Shaping words, actions, thoughts, and reactions into evidence when it is not so obvious takes practice. Show students how to use weaker evidence to their advantage.

- Help students recognize when their evidence is too similar. Using class discussions, exemplars, and games, demonstrate evidence that is too similar or that lacks enough distinctive variety. Also, having students weigh evidence encourages them to seek out more evidence, which could also help resolve the problem.

LESSON
16

Writing From the RACE Planner

Demonstrate ways in which students can use their RACE Real-Time Planner, with its thrifty use of words, to compose complete and fluent sentences.

Quick Start: How can I write from my RACE Real-Time Planner?

Making Connections

Tell students that their RACE Real-Time Planner captures their good ideas and evidence. Now, they will turn these ideas into complete sentences so readers can easily understand them. They will start with the introduction, move to the body paragraphs, and then end with the conclusion.

Display "Writing From a Planner" (page 136) on the board and hand out copies to show students some quick and easy ways to write from their RACE Real-Time Planner.

Close-Up #1: Humpty Dumpty & Little Boy Blue

Display question #31 (page 131) on the board. Say: *Let's revisit question #31 about Humpty Dumpty and Little Boy Blue and see how we can use write from our RACE Real-Time Planner.* Model as you think-aloud. (See response exemplar, next page and online.)

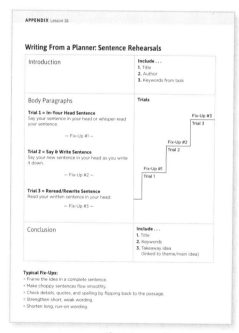

(See Appendix, page 136.)

- Let's start with the introduction. Recall that we used an *I* as the only note for our introduction in our RACE Real-Time Planner. That's because the introduction should be simple to write—no need for notes! Introductions include easy-to-find details: title, author, and keywords from the task. Remember, do NOT use abbreviations (e.g., initials) or other short forms of words when you write your answer.

I = (titles, genres, authors + key ideas from task paraphrased in own words)		
(RA1) A lesson both teach is . . . make smart choices.		**(C1)** HD = makes foolish choice to sit on wall **(C2)** LBB = chooses to sleep instead of work
(RA2) The lesson is taught when . . . their unwise choices backfire.		**(C1)** HD makes a foolish choice, sits on wall, falls, & can't be put back together **(C2)** LBB isn't at job, is asleep instead, cows & sheep wander away, people look for him

...e added)

31 "Humpty Dumpty" and "Little Boy Blue" are children's nursery rhymes that were written long ago. Nursery rhymes are simple stories that were often used to teach young children lessons. What is a lesson that "Humpty Dumpty" and "Little Boy Blue" teach children? How does each story teach that lesson? Use details from both stories to support your response.

In your response, be sure to:
- describe a lesson that both stories teach.
- explain how the lesson is taught in both stories.
- use details from both stories.

You may plan your writing for question 31 on the blank page provided (not shown).

Humpty Dumpty

Humpty Dumpty sat on a wall.
Humpty Dumpty had a great fall.
All the King's horses and all the King's men
Couldn't put Humpty Dumpty together again.

Little Boy Blue

Little Boy Blue, come blow your horn!
The sheep's in the meadow,
The cow's in the corn.
Where is that boy who looks after the sheep?
He's under a haystack, fast asleep.

"Humpty Dumpty" and "Little Boy Blue" are children's nursery rhymes that were written many years ago. Nursery rhymes are simple stories used to teach young children lessons. Both of these teach an important lesson.

A lesson both stories teach is that children should make smart choices. I know this because Humpty Dumpty makes a foolish choice by sitting on a wall. Little Boy Blue also makes an unwise decision, choosing to sleep instead of work.

The lesson is taught in each story when the character's decision backfires. In "Humpty Dumpty," Humpty, an egg, makes a foolish choice to sit on a wall. This is unwise because next he has a "great fall" and breaks. Also, the text states that the King's horses and men "couldn't put Humpty back together again." In "Little Boy Blue," this lesson is taught when Little Boy Blue makes an unwise decision to sleep under a haystack instead of doing his job. First, he doesn't blow his horn to keep the sheep and cows from wandering away. Also, people are looking for him and asking, "Where is the boy?"

The lesson in the nursery rhymes "Humpty Dumpty" and "Little Boy Blue" is that children need to make smart choices. This lesson was good a long time ago and still for today.

(Available online.)

- While this basic introduction may lack a sense of writing craft and voice, it is nonetheless a solid, three-sentence introduction. This simple introduction has all of the basics except the authors, which were not provided. In lessons that follow, we'll see how we can improve it.

- Let's move to the first body paragraph. Shaping our notes into sentences involves trial and error. We may need to do a first, second, or even third try to get things right. The Writing From a Planner handout helps. While it may seem time-consuming to "rehearse" a sentence three times, our brains move the process along at super speed! Also, rehearsing your sentence so it sounds just right is a skill that improves with practice.

- The first sentence (RA1) becomes our topic sentence. It includes the restated question and our inference. C1 launches our evidence. (Note: You may wish to use an evidence starter and revisit the transition words in Chapter 2, page 58.) Then we'll connect our second piece of evidence, C2. Each time we construct a sentence, we'll want to rehearse and adjust it until it sounds right in every way—it says what we mean and will be understood that way by our readers.

- We'll use this same process for the next question. Our answer for this question becomes the next body paragraph. Working through the trials and fix-up in Writing From a Planner is an important skill to help us take ideas from our planner and construct them into complete sentences on our paper.

- Finally, we'll write the conclusion, which will be the final paragraph. Recall that we wrote C as the only note for our conclusion in our RACE Real-Time Planner. Like the introduction, the conclusion should be simple to write. In addition to the title, author, and keywords from the task, we write a meaningful takeaway.

- Now, we'll want to proofread for CUPS (capitalization, understanding/usage, punctuation, spelling). Even though we have carefully rehearsed and used fix-ups in our sentences, a CUPS review helps make sure our essay is error-free!

Note: The response exemplar shown is a very basic yet thorough essay. In the next lesson, we'll learn some quick and easy strategies to add CRAFT.

Close-Up #2: When Looks Matter & It Came From the Mud

Display question #32 (page 133) on the board. Say to students: *Let's try another example. This task is to write an essay that uses evidence from the two passages. Although the task doesn't have question prompts, we can adapt our skills easily.*

- Let's start with the introduction, for which we used an *I* to note its place in our RACE Real-Time Planner. Again, we just need to include easy-to-find details, such as the titles, authors (not provided in these articles), and keywords from the task.

- Next, let's look at the first body paragraph. The first sentence (RA1) becomes our topic sentence. It includes our first claim to support the argument in the task (fish and mammals' features help them survive). C1 launches our evidence, then we'll connect our second piece of evidence (C2).

- Repeat this same process for the next two paragraphs.

Have students use their RACE Real-Time Planners from the last lesson to write the rest of their extended response, as well as the conclusion. Remind them that the conclusion is just like the introduction, but with a meaningful takeaway added. (The thumbnail at right shows a sample response.)

Using both Close-Ups, guide students to see that:

I = (titles, genres, authors + key ideas from task paraphrased in own words)

(RA1) first is the pangolin (P1) covered in scales	(C1) covered from head to tail (C2) body armor protects from predators, like tigers with teeth
(RA2) second is the mudskipper (P2) body parts help it survive in water & land	(C1) fins & tails for movement (C2) gills to breathe
(RA3) third is body p	

C = (circle bac
E = (edit remin

32 Scientists who study fish and mammals explain that they look the way they do often because their survival depends on it. In other words, these creatures may have special, easy-to-see features that help them survive in their environments. Write an essay that explains the features that some fish and mammals have that help them survive. Be sure to use facts and details from both passages to support your explanation.

Be sure to include:
- an introduction
- support for your ideas using information from the passages
- a conclusion that is relevant

Your response should be in the form of a multiple-paragraph essay. You may plan your writing for question 32 on the blank page provided (not shown).

Scientists explain that some fish and mammals look the way they do because their survival depends on it. After reading "When Looks Matter" and "It Came From the Mud," I learned about one mammal and two fishes that have some special features to help them survive in their environments.

First, the pangolin is a mammal completely covered in scales. According to passage 1, it looks like it is wearing a coat of armor! It is covered from head to tail because it has to fend off predators. For example, tigers are one of its predators. The pangolin's armor keeps it safe against tigers' and other predators' teeth.

Second, the mudskipper lives on land and in water (passage 2), so its special features help it survive in both environments. Its fins and tail help it move in the mud. It can even use its tail to jump. Also, the mudskipper uses its gills to breathe. All of these features help it survive on land and in water.

Third, the seahorse is another creature with strange body parts that help it find food. According to passage 2, the seahorse can suck up tiny shrimp with its snout. Likewise, it can grab onto plants with its tail.

No doubt these three creatures have special features that help them survive. The pangolin fends off predators with its coat of armor, the mudskipper can survive on land and in water with its special body parts, and the seahorse uses its strange features to find food. Scientists are right when they say that an animal's survival sometimes depends on the way it looks!

(Available online.)

- writing from the RACE Real-Time Planner is quick and easy.
- the conclusion and introduction are a lot alike and include easy-to-find details.

- the body paragraphs, which include cited evidence ideas (C1 and C2), are easily shaped into complete, understandable sentences.
- using rehearsals and fix-ups so sentences express their ideas—just as they intend— are helpful strategies.

Quick Close

Tell students: *A well-written extended response is not difficult, especially when we write from a RACE Real-Time Planner. Our planner reminds us to hold a spot for the introduction and conclusion, which we'll compose in real-time. We simply use easy-to-find details in both to make writing them an easy-to-do part of the task. Writing from our planner notes is also easy when we use our rehearsal and fix-up strategies. For both, we'll need to reread and listen to our sentences. Making sure we've said what we mean—so we can show what we know—is key!*

Independent Readiness Survey

Gauge students' comfort level with writing their extended responses from their RACE Real-Time Planner. Read the numbered statements below and have students respond in one of three ways:
- Thumbs up if they agree
- Thumbs down if they disagree and want more guided practice with a teacher
- Thumbs midway if they almost agree but would like to work with a partner

1. I know what details to include in an introduction, and I know how to locate and use them effectively.
2. I know how to rehearse and fix-up the sentences I write from the ideas in my RACE Real-Time Planner.
3. I know what details to include in a conclusion, and I know how to add a takeaway idea that makes my conclusion thoughtful.
4. I can independently write from my RACE Real-Time Planner so that my ideas are expressed in complete and understandable sentences—just the way I intend.

Teaching Notes
- Allow time for students to learn how to shape a fluent sentence from brief ideas, letting them know that this process may require several "takes."

- In the RACE Real-Time Planner, students use placeholders for key components of their essays, such as the introduction and conclusion. Now, they will call to action and apply the writing techniques they have been taught during their regular classroom writing instruction.

- There are many different and equally good ways to "paragraph" an extended response. Students can use a format suggested by the task or decide if another way works better, such as splitting one large paragraph into two smaller ones (especially when a task involves two passages). They can make this decision once they begin to see the volume of their writing.

- You may wish to suggest a more basic paragraph structure to help scaffold students who are developing their skills in organizing and writing extended responses. You may also wish to suggest a scaffolded way to organize paragraphs for struggling writers. You can put these scaffolds in place for students until their writing skills with extended responses strengthen.

- Learning to write complete sentences from idea notes takes practice. Jockeying between oral and written rehearsal helps students develop this skill. Repeated readings are often necessary to keep track of ideas as they move from thoughts into written expression.

- Students can check off parts of their RACE Real-Time Planner as they shape a sentence for each component. This will help keep them on track.

- You may wish to dictate student ideas during practice. This helps students evaluate (1) if their sentences reflect their intended meaning and (2) if a reader would understand the sentence as written.

- Encourage students to "listen" to their writing as they turn notes into written expression. They can practice this through paired or group writing activities.

- When writing from their planner, students will still need to flip back to the passages. This will help them find the author's name, spell words correctly, refine ideas, use quotes, locate the paragraphs, and ensure the accuracy of their ideas.

- Modeling how to move from a planner to a written response greatly helps students grasp this process. Lead whole-class demonstrations that actively involve students in thinking through how to shape ideas into sentences.

- Modeling the planning and the writing together actively with students also gives them an idea of their pacing.

- About 45 to 60 minutes to complete writing an extended response is a relatively reliable estimation and can improve with practice. Although these kinds of tasks may be untimed, student stamina must be considered.

- Modeling a "takeaway" to include in a conclusion takes practice. Often, the takeaway is a theme or a main idea. Help students recognize this and then apply this as they write a conclusion.

 LESSON 17

Revising and Editing for CRAFT

Show students how to apply their CUPS skills (from Chapter 2), blend the revise and edit stages together, and target their adjustments for CRAFT.

Quick Start: How can the CRAFT strategy improve our extended response?

Making Connections

Tell students: *We've already learned how CUPS—capitalization, understanding, punctuation, and spelling—can help us edit our short responses (Lesson 12). Now, let's learn about CRAFT.*

Explain that CRAFT stands for:

    C = Cohesion
    R = Repetition
    A = Artful word choice
    F = Fluency
    T = Transitions

It is a way of looking closely at the words, sentences, paragraphs, and the whole extended response. CRAFT reminds us about the craft of writing—the skill, style, and effectiveness of the way we communicate our ideas. This quick and easy CRAFT strategy strengthens our lengthier real-time writing. Some students think it's a quick real-time revision process. Interesting!

31 "Humpty Dumpty" and "Little Boy Blue" are children's <u>nursery rhymes</u> that were written long ago. Nursery rhymes are <u>simple stories</u> that were often <u>used to teach young children lessons.</u> [What] is a lesson that "Humpty Dumpty" and "Little Boy Blue" teach children[?] [How] does each story teach that lesson[?] Use details from <u>both</u> stories to support your response.

In your response, be sure to:

- describe a lesson that both stories teach.
- explain how the lesson is taught in both stories.
- use details from both stories.

You may plan your writing for question 31 on the blank page provided (not shown).

Humpty Dumpty

Humpty Dumpty sat on a wall.
Humpty Dumpty had a great fall.
All the King's horses and all the King's men
Couldn't put Humpty together again.

Little Boy Blue

Little Boy Blue, come blow your horn!
The sheep's in the meadow,
The cow's in the corn.
Where is that boy who looks after the sheep?
He's under a haystack, fast asleep.

"Humpty Dumpty" and "Little Boy Blue" are **well-known** children's nursery rhymes that were written ~~many years~~ **centuries** ago. Nursery rhymes are ~~simple~~ **basic** stories used to teach young children **life** lessons. Both of these teach ~~an important~~ **critical** lesson **easily and quickly.**

A lesson both stories teach is that children should make smart choices. I know this because Humpty Dumpty makes a foolish choice by sitting on a wall. Little Boy Blue also makes ~~an unwise~~ **poor** decision, choosing to sleep instead of work.

The lesson is taught in each story when the character's decision backfires. In "Humpty Dumpty," **the main character, Humpty, is an egg,** ~~makes a foolish choice to~~ **who foolishly** sits on a wall. This is ~~unwise~~ **not so smart** because next he has a "great fall" and breaks. ~~Also, the text states~~ **Moreover, the evidence shows** that the King's horses and men "couldn't put Humpty back together again." In "Little Boy Blue," this lesson is taught when Little Boy Blue ~~makes an unwise decision~~ **doesn't use good thinking and decides** to sleep under a haystack instead of doing his job. First, he doesn't blow his horn to keep the sheep and cows from wandering away. ~~Also~~ **In addition to this,** people are looking for him and asking, "Where is the boy?"

The lesson in the nursery rhymes "Humpty Dumpty" and "Little Boy Blue" is that children need to make smart choices. This lesson was good a long time ago and still for today.

There is no doubt that ~~T~~ the lesson in the **centuries-old** nursery rhymes "Humpty Dumpty" and "Little Boy Blue" is that children ~~need to make~~ **benefit from making** smart choices. This **quick and easy** lesson was good a long time ago and ~~still~~ **remains critical** ~~for~~ today.

(Available online.)

Close-Up #1: Humpty Dumpty & Little Boy Blue

Display question #31 with the sample response (available online) on the board. Say to students: *In our last lesson, we wrote an extended response from our RACE Real-Time Planner. Let's see how adding CRAFT helps kick up our response.*

- Let's begin by looking at the introduction. Recall that an introduction includes three must-haves: title, author, keywords from the task.
- This basic introduction is good and serves the purpose of introducing the main ideas. One big problem is that it's boring. It doesn't flow well, and our readers may not find it enjoyable. Let's explore some CRAFT revisions. Let's revise/edit for A (artfulness of word choice) and F (fluency) to improve this basic yet boring introduction.

Model how to make a few edits to make the paragraph flow better, thinking aloud as you make the changes. (The boldface type in the sample response at left offers some options.) Modeling, using boldface or italicized alternatives, is a quick way for students to grasp the powerful impact of a few or very small changes.

- We can add some adjectives and descriptive phrases to tighten meaning (*well-known, centuries, basic, life, critical*) and adverbs to better describe our ideas (*easily and quickly*). We can improve the fluency by selecting words that fit nicely together and extend ideas smoothly (stories are *well-known, centuries-old,* and teach *critical* lessons *easily*). All of these changes enrich the introduction and invite the reader to engage.

- Now let's revisit paragraphs 2 and 3 of the body of our essay and make some CRAFT revisions. First, let's look at repetition. The most frequent (yet the easiest to quick fix) repetition is with transitions. Here, the student uses *Also* to add ideas. The repetition of *Also* is an easy fix. It is a basic transition. We can easily fix this by swapping in another basic transition, such as *in addition*. We can also use stronger CRAFT transitions, such as those on "More Transitions & Transitional Phrases" (page 137). Using a variety of transitions results in a stronger response.

- Another easy fix is with repeated words or phrases. Often changing one or two words improves the response.

- Finally, we can make other fluency improvements. For example, the following sentence in the second body paragraph is a little clumsy:

  In "Humpty Dumpty," Humpty, an egg, makes a foolish choice to sit on a wall.

  We might wish to go back and make it more fluent. For example:

  *In "Humpty Dumpty," **the main character**, Humpty, **is** an egg, **who foolishly** sits on a wall.*

- Now, let's review the conclusion for CRAFT. Recall that the conclusion includes these must-haves: title, author, and genre (if available); keywords from the task and answers; and a final, takeaway idea.

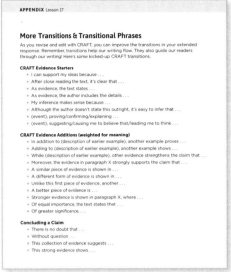

(See Appendix, page 137.)

- Although this basic conclusion serves the purpose of reviewing the main ideas, we can improve our response through some simple CRAFT revision (shown in bold).

- Finally, let's take a broad sweep over the entire response and check for cohesion, or the way our answer hangs together.

  ✔ Complex ideas are well presented, organized, supported, and balanced.
  ✔ Ideas are framed in a well-written introduction and conclusion.
  ✔ Our response shows skill, style, and is error-free.
  ✔ Repetition problems have been fixed.
  ✔ Word choices are careful and artful, some even stretching beyond grade level.
  ✔ Ideas flow well.
  ✔ The transitions guide the reader along.

  Our CRAFT revisions are complete!

From Close-Up #1, students can see that:

- CRAFT is a real-time way to revise and edit at the same time.
- one approach is to start small by looking for quick-fix problems.
- they can easily improve overuse of basic transitions and repetition. Word choice and fluency come next. Finally, they should take a broad look at the cohesion of their response.
- another approach is to target areas that address their challenge areas.

Close-Up #2: When Looks Matter & It Came From the Mud

Display question #32 with the sample response (available online) on the board and hand out copies. Say to students: *Let's look at the other extended response from our last lesson.*

- Let's begin by looking at the introduction, which again must include these three pieces of information: title, author, and keywords from the task.

- This basic introduction is good and serves the purpose of introducing the main ideas. One problem is that it's boring and relies too heavily on words from the task. Let's explore some CRAFT revisions that will make it more enjoyable and add a balance of original words.

32 Scientists who study <u>fish and mammals</u> explain that they look the way they do often because their <u>survival depends on it</u>. In other words, these creatures may have special, easy-to-see features that help them survive in their environments. Write an <u>essay</u> that <u>explains</u> the <u>features</u> that <u>some fish and mammals have</u> that help them <u>survive</u>. Be sure to use facts and details from both passages to support your explanation.

Be sure to include:
- an <u>introduction</u>
- <u>support</u> for your ideas using information from the passages
- a <u>conclusion</u> that is relevant

Your response should be in the form of a <u>multiple-paragraph essay</u>. You may plan your writing for question 32 on the blank page provided (not shown).

Scientists ~~explain~~ **help us understand** that some fishes and mammals ~~look the way they do~~ **may have strange-looking features** because their survival depends on it. After reading "When Looks Matter" and "It Came From the Mud," I learned about ~~one mammal and two fishes that have some special~~ **three creatures whose ugly** features ~~to~~ help them survive ~~in their environments~~.

~~First~~ **To begin,** the pangolin is a mammal completely covered in scales. According to passage 1, it looks like it is wearing a coat of armor! It is covered from head to tail because it has to fend off predators. For example, tigers are one of its predators. The pangolin's armor keeps it safe against tigers' and other predators' **sharp** teeth.

~~Second~~ **In addition to the pangolin, the mudskipper has odd survival features.** ~~↑~~The mudskipper lives on land and in water (passage 2), so its special features help it survive in both environments. Its fins and tail help it move in the mud. It can even use its tail to jump. ~~Also,~~ **In addition,** the mudskipper uses its gills to breathe. ~~All of these features help it survive on land and in water.~~

~~Third~~ **Unlike the mudskipper, which uses its features to move and breathe,** the seahorse is ~~another~~ a creature with strange body parts that help it find food. ~~According to passage~~ **As stated in passage** 2, the seahorse can suck up tiny shrimp with its snout. ~~Also~~ **Furthermore,** it can grab onto plants with its tail.

<u>Without question, scientists are right!</u> ~~No doubt that~~ ~~↑~~These three creatures have special features that help them survive. The pangolin ~~fends off~~ **hinders** predators with its coat of armor, the mudskipper ~~can easily~~ survive**s** on land and in water with its special body parts, and the seahorse uses its strange features to find food. ~~Scientists are right when they say that a fish or mammal's survival sometimes depends on the way it looks!~~

(Available online.)

Model how to make a few edits to make the paragraph flow better, thinking aloud as you make the changes. (The boldface type in the sample response at left offers some options.)

- We can add some phrases in our own words (*help us understand that*) and stronger adjectives (*strange-looking/ugly*). We can improve fluency by replacing the phrase "one mammal and two fishes" with "three creatures." It is less wordy, moves the idea along, and avoids repeating ideas already in the first sentence. All of these changes enrich the introduction and invite the reader to engage.

Have students revisit the rest of the essay and make some CRAFT revisions on their own. Remind them to pay attention to repetitions, keeping in mind that the most frequent repetition, yet easiest to fix, is with transitions.

Allow students time to edit the other paragraphs in the extended response. Then discuss edits and revisions they made and why.

Quick Close

Tell students: *The CRAFT Strategy helps us improve the quality of our extended responses. It does this by helping us focus our fix-up efforts in five areas:*

C = Cohesion
R = Repetition
A = Artful word choice
F = Fluency
T = Transitions

Making sure you demonstrate your writing skill and style—together with your knowledge—is key!

Independent Readiness Survey

Gauge students' comfort level with using CRAFT to revise and edit their extended responses. Read the numbered statements below and have students respond in one of three ways:

- Thumbs up if they agree
- Thumbs down if they disagree and want more guided practice with a teacher
- Thumbs midway if they almost agree but would like to work with a partner

1. I know what each letter in CRAFT stands for.
2. I know how to check over my extended response for problems with cohesion, repetition, artful word choice, fluency, and transitions.
3. I can independently make some quick fixes to improve cohesion, repetition, artful word choice, fluency, and transitions in my extended response.

Teaching Notes

- Teaching CRAFT in reverse (TFARC) adds novelty to the strategy and better aligns with addressing smaller to larger elements of an extended response. Students can learn the terms and techniques first and then apply them in reverse order.

- You may wish to target one or two CRAFT techniques, such as fluency or transitions, that will significantly improve a student's response. Scaffolding students' skill in this manner helps them build their unique style.

- Consider assigning groups of students to tackle one element of the CRAFT technique and share their improvement ideas.

- Encourage students to select two or three favorite basic and two or three favorite CRAFT transitions. Collections of transitional words and phrases can easily be found on the internet. Students also enjoy making up their own transitional phrases.

- Model quick-fix revisions selectively to help students gauge how to use their real-time revision skills effectively. For example, replacing multiple words in a single sentence with artful alternatives may be overkill. Selecting one or two to replace among several sentences is more powerful and more in keeping with the intent of the CRAFT revision/editing strategy.

- CRAFT revisions/edits are intended as real-time quick fixes to improve glaring problems or pauses that prevent a reader from remaining engaged and moving swiftly along. Used sparingly and in this manner, CRAFT is useful for real-time writing.

- Remind students that they will also likely need to apply CUPS to their CRAFT revisions.

- Eventually, students will internalize the CRAFT techniques and apply them automatically in real time, as they compose their responses. Until then, they can practice by erasing/deleting and changing words or adding information with carets to master this type of advanced real-time revision/editing.

- Real-time revising for cohesion problems are often challenging, especially if additional text must be added to clarify, support, or balance ideas. Students can add one or two sentences using a caret, yet it is better to have them craft a stronger sentence from the start. Think of CRAFT as polish to already-drafted ideas.

- Practicing the CRAFT techniques on guided writing samples (teacher- and student-generated) is effective and timesaving. Students do not need to construct an original response but instead can focus on CRAFT changes.

- Remind students that they can use their CRAFT strategy to improve all of their writing. This will help them own and tailor the process to build their own writing style.

CHAPTER 4

Quick & Easy Strategies for Moving Beyond Structured Writing

The ideas, lessons, and resources in this book present effective close-reading and structured, real-time writing strategies. Used together, these strategies help students tackle tasks that call upon their unified skill of reading and writing literacy. While this covers a vast scope of literary activity, the focus of this book has been on the type of response writing most often associated with test-taking. However, there are many other ways in which these same strategies benefit students as they engage in other forms of combined reading and writing tasks—research, information/explanatory, and opinion/arguments, and even narrative.

In this chapter, we'll take a step forward and look at how to move students beyond formulas and a structured approach to writing by adapting these skills in order to move them in a direction that is more authentic and unique to each student. The lessons in this chapter provide some direction to help students seek and explore ways to shape their response writing so it reflects their unique voice and style. These strategies are:

- Stray & Play
- Add More & Explore
- Develop Voice by Expanding Choice

Note: While it is very important to help students build a sense of style and voice, it's also important not to misguide them. If their responses will be evaluated by specific criteria in a rubric, make sure to convey this to them. They should understand the criteria in grade-appropriate terms.

Can-Do-It-My-Way Attitude

Keep in mind that the strategies covered in this book are best considered a good beginning. They help support students when their analytical reading and writing skills are merged together and called into action under time (and stamina) constraints. There comes a point, however, when it makes sense to extend their "Can-Do Attitude" into a "Can-Do-It-My-Way Attitude."

To provide some direction to extend student skill, it might be helpful to think in terms of three paths or avenues.

1. Stray & Play Encourage students to move away from a structured approach to reading, thinking, and writing responses. Recall from the first chapter that the way students text-mark a passage shows some common elements and some unique elements. This reflects their shared and unique interactions with the text. The same holds true for how students will interact with writing tasks. Some may confidently "shortcut" the planning process and use a streamlined approach that aligns with their unique thinking processes. They may also stray from the formula that guides the content of their response. For example, they may wish to add multiple details of evidence, even though they're asked for only two, if that's what their inner academic voice suggests (providing they have the time and stamina to do so). Students may also arrange their ideas in a strategic order that differs from the way a question is asked. While there are others, these "strays & plays" are often the first steps a student takes in moving beyond the structure to take charge of his or her response.

This lesson includes various "style surveys," which enable students to reflect on their own style and to gauge how best to move away from structure and toward an independent take-charge mindset for responding to prompted tasks that involve reading and writing.

2. Add More & Explore Introduce and foster the use of creative writing techniques in students' written responses. You may need to set some mild parameters, but using figurative language, such as a well-placed simile, metaphor, personification, or idiom, in a response can showcase students' style and originality. It can also reveal their understanding. Likewise, students can experiment with imagery by adding sensory details to help readers see, feel, hear, taste, or smell key ideas. Finally, word techniques, such as interjections and onomatopoeia, as well as varied sentence structures may also boost not only students' responses but also their interest in exploring other ways to energize their writing.

Many of these figurative language and creative skills are often taught through different units of instruction, such as poetry or creative writing. Provide students with multiple opportunities to practice these skills by incorporating them in morning routines, "ticket" activities, letter writing, and more.

3. Develop Voice by Expanding Choice Ask three people their definition of *voice* and expect three different answers. However, what remains consistent is the idea that voice captures the unique sound and personality of the writer. Most experts agree that voice stems from many factors, such as word choice, sentence construction, rhythm, and tone. In this lesson, we'll explore how students can make choices to express their ideas their way—and with confidence.

Encourage students to respond to literature and informational texts authentically (as in a writer's response journal) to help them develop their response-writing voice. (See "Routine Response Writing Prompt," page 138.)

(See Appendix, page 138.)

Stray & Play

Encourage students to discover and develop their own text-marking, planning, and paragraphing and ordering styles.

Quick Start: You've learned, practiced, and independently applied reading and writing strategies to help you answer text-based prompts. What's next? Develop your unique style!

Making Connections

Tell students: *One way to develop your unique style is to "Stray & Play."* Stray *means "to move away from something." In this lesson, you'll move away from the structures you've learned.* Play *means to explore your own ways of doing things.*

One way to stray that we've already explored is with text-marking. The way each of you will interact with the text is going to be unique.

Close-Up #1: Developing a Text-Marking Style

Display two samples of text markings (available online) on the board. Say to students: *Let's take a look at how two different students text-marked the same passage. Do you notice markings that are the same? How about ones that are different? We expect this. We all interact with a text differently and will express our ideas differently. To help figure out your*

(Available online.)

Sample from Lesson 5 Close-Up #1

text-marking style, explore what you do. Gauge if it works well or if you think you may need to make changes. Hand out copies of "What's My Text-Marking Style?" (page 139) and give students a few minutes to answer the survey.

Close-Up #2: Developing a Planning Style

Next, display two versions of the RACE Real-Time Planners (available online) on the board and say: *Another way to stray is with the planning process you use to write a short or extended answer. How much planning do you need to show what you know? Notice how these two students planned their extended responses in different ways, even though their answers are similar. They've even used some of the same details. We expect this. Students will use their planning tools differently, and they will also express their ideas within the planning tools differently. To help figure out your planning style, explore what you do. Gauge if it works well or if you think you may need to make changes.* Hand out copies of "What's My Planning Style?" (page 140) and give students a few minutes to answer the survey.

(See Appendix, page 139.)

(See Appendix, page 140.)

(Available online.)

Close-Up #3: Developing a Flexible Formula Style

Display the sample response for "An Extreme Adventure" question #3 (available online) on the board. Say: *A third way to stray is with the content you include in your answer. You can move away from familiar formulas, such as RACE or RADDE, to show your take on things. This means you can begin your response in a way that makes sense to you. For example, this student could have started her answer with: "Paragraphs 4 and 5 show us many things about Alex." That would be in keeping with the R (restate the question) in RACE. Instead, she goes directly to A (answer) by opening up her response with: "Alex is very talented and can handle stress very well."*

---

3 In "An Extreme Adventure," what do paragraphs 4 and 5 show us about Alex? Use two details from the article to support your answer.

Alex is very talented and can handle stress very well. I know this because in paragraph 4 it says that he has to know five dancers' routines and be able to perform each of them flawlessly. Only someone with real talent can do that. In paragraph 5, Alex admits that "it's a little stressful," but he adds that "it never becomes stale." He says that with a laugh. That tells me he handles stress quite well. Alex proves that being a swing dancer is indeed an "extreme adventure."

(Available online.)

---

30 In *The Wizard of Oz* by L. Frank Baum, Dorothy's feelings change from the beginning to the end of the story. What causes Dorothy's feelings to change? Use details from the story to support your response.

In your response, be sure to
- describe how Dorothy feels in the beginning of the story
- describe how Dorothy feels at the end of the story
- explain what causes Dorothy's feelings to change
- use details from the story to support your response

You may plan your writing for question 30 on the blank page provided (not shown).

In L. Frank Baum's *The Wizard of Oz*, Dorothy's feelings change from the beginning to the end of the story.

In the beginning of the story, Dorothy felt unhappy and restless. Her dog, Toto, had been taken away from her. Even though Toto snuck back home, Dorothy was still very sad and ran away from home. She even asked Professor Marvel to take her to Europe with him! Clearly, Dorothy wasn't happy and wished to leave her home and family behind.

Dorothy did get her wish when a tornado picked her and Toto up and brought them to the land of Oz. Here, she faced many challenges and learned some important lessons. For example, she learned about the importance of teamwork and what it's like to belong to a caring team. The Oz characters were like her family. She also learned that what she really wanted more than anything was to get back home to her real family.

At the end of the story, Dorothy got back home from Oz, and she was happy and thankful for all that she had, especially her family and home. She shows this by hugging everyone and telling them how much she missed them. Adding to this, she said she wouldn't look any farther than her backyard for her heart's desire. This means she had everything she wanted at home.

Dorothy's feelings changed in the story because she learned it was important to have a caring family team. Her aunt and uncle cared for her a lot, and she realized that she cared for them just as much. Dorothy's trip to Oz helped her figure out her true feelings.

(Available online.)

Another way to stray is to include as many details as you feel you need to support your good ideas, but in keeping with the task directions. So even though a task may ask for "two details," if you feel three or four details would strengthen your answer, go for it.

Finally, it also means you can conclude your answer in a way that makes sense to you. Notice how the student used the title of the passage in her conclusion.

Close-Up #4: Developing a Paragraphing and Order Style

Tell students that a fourth way to stray is by deciding how to organize their ideas in a response. One way is to take charge of how many paragraphs to use. We've explored this in Lesson 13 with our RACE Real-Time Planner. Another way is by deciding in which order to answer different parts of a multi-question task.

Display the sample response for *The Wizard of Oz* question #30 (available online) on the board and say: *This prompt requires an answer to three different questions. It lists the questions in bullet format, one after another. The student responded to all of the bullets, but chose to answer them in a different order—one that was guided by his take-charge thinking.*

Point out that the task asks about how a character felt at the beginning of the story, how she felt at the end of the story, and what caused her feelings to change. Instead of answering the question in the same order as the bullet points, this student followed the story's chronological order in his response. Ordering his answer this way was more in line with his thinking.

Tell students: *To help figure out your take-charge style, explore what you do. Gauge if it works well or if you think you may need to make changes.* Hand out copies of "Am I Taking Charge of My Answers?" (page 141) and give students a few minutes to answer the survey.

APPENDIX Lesson 1B

Am I Taking Charge of My Answers?

Are your good ideas—instead of a formula—shaping your answer?
Take this survey to find out.

1. Do I start my answer in a way that makes sense to me? Place an X on the scale.

Usually		Sometimes		Always
☐ 1	☐ 2	☐ 3	☐ 4	☐ 5

2. Do I support my ideas in a way that makes sense to me? Place an X on the scale.

Usually		Sometimes		Always
☐ 1	☐ 2	☐ 3	☐ 4	☐ 5

3. Do I conclude my answer in a way that makes sense to me? Place an X on the scale.

Usually		Sometimes		Always
☐ 1	☐ 2	☐ 3	☐ 4	☐ 5

4. Based on my answers above, are there any changes I can make to improve my take-charge action?

5. Are there other ways I take charge of the formulas (RACE and others) that show my unique style?

(See Appendix, page 141.)

Quick Close

Say to students: *The Stray & Play strategy is one way to move beyond a structured way of responding to tasks. It's also a way to explore your good ideas and take charge of what ideas to include and how you want to express them. It works with text-marking (the way your read and interact with a text), as well as with the way you plan and write your response.*

Independent Readiness Survey

Gauge students' comfort level with using the Stray & Play strategy in their responses.
Read the numbered statements below and have students respond in one of three ways:

- Thumbs up if they agree
- Thumbs down if they disagree and want more guided practice with a teacher
- Thumbs midway if they almost agree but would like to work with a partner

1. I can explore ways to find my own text-marking style.
2. I can explore ways to find my own planning style.
3. I can explore ways to develop, organize, and take charge of my response.

Teaching Notes

- The playfulness of the Stray & Play strategies motivates students to assume greater independence during practice. Help them gauge and monitor their progress as needed.

- Celebrate students' successes and encourage them to persevere through challenges. Students will develop a level of independence with these reading, writing, and thinking strategies at different times and at different rates. Some cheerleading will go a long way.

- You may wish to use sample test exemplars to show students a variety of acceptable ways to answer questions. Share ideas on the depth and scope of different answers in class discussions.

- Some caution may be necessary to ensure students' use of the Stray & Play strategies aligns with task directions as well as with rubrics used to evaluate student responses. Avoid mismatches between task requirements and students' interpretations of directions.

- Students may wish to routinely survey and track their progress using the "What's My Style?" surveys in this lesson. To track their progress, they can create charts, such as Venn diagrams, to compare their responses over time.

- If students must include an inference in a short response, add a question about this to question #1 of the What's My Planning Style? survey. For example: "Does my planning help me make an inference?" would be a question that could help them self-assess the value of their planning. To keep track of their ideas, students often benefit from making their thinking transparent in a plan.

- Students can examine the quality of their work as they Stray & Play. For example, those who choose to write a response without planning can rate the quality of two answers—one with a plan and one without. To add novelty and engagement, have students work in pairs or teams to help them self-monitor their work.

- Students who have recurring problems with using these strategies (e.g., incomplete responses, missed tasks, and so on) can easily return to a structured approach or put other self-monitoring systems in place. Student' responses must always reflect their skills.

- Helping students build their independence is a path to helping them find their voice. Although some caution is necessary to get there, the benefit is worth it.

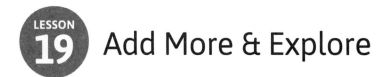

LESSON 19 Add More & Explore

Help students explore various writing techniques, such as figurative language and imagery, as well as word use and sentence structures.

Quick Start: You've learned to Stray & Play in our last lesson. What's next in terms of developing your unique style? Add More & Explore!

Making Connections

Tell students: *In this lesson, you'll be adding a few "high-power" techniques to your writing. We'll explore:*

- *figurative language (simile, metaphor, personification, idiom)*
- *imagery (using sensory details)*
- *interjection and onomatopoeia (playful use of word sounds)*
- *sentence structure (combining sentences and changing sentence beginnings)*

Display "Creative Writing Techniques" (page 142) on the board and discuss with the class. Invite students to provide examples of each.

Close-Up #1: Humpty Dumpty & Little Boy Blue

Display the sample response to question #31 (available online) on the board. Say to students: *Let's take a close look at our extended response from "Humpty Dumpty" and "Little Boy Blue."*

- One way to use figurative language is in a closing sentence of a paragraph, such as in paragraph 2. Here, we can add a simile comparing Humpty Dumpty and Little Boy Blue's choices to the character of the Big Bad Wolf in "Little Red Riding Hood." This simile works because we're comparing bad choices to a bad character. This simile also works because we use an example from a fairy tale, which is like a nursery rhyme—both are written for children. Also, the placement at the end of the paragraph nicely sums up the point that both characters made very bad choices.

- We can add the playful use of the word sound *BOOM* to the topic sentence of the third paragraph. This works because we are adding detail that enriches the sound of a "backfire." This example also creates imagery. Adding the word *BOOM* helps the reader hear the backfire.

- We can also add a closing sentence to this paragraph that uses personification. Here, *trouble* has the human characteristic of being able to awaken Little Boy Blue.

- Finally, let's try a sentence structure change. In our conclusion, we can change the order of our sentence beginning. This change adds sentence variety to our response. It also focuses on the lesson of the nursery rhymes. Both strengthen the response.

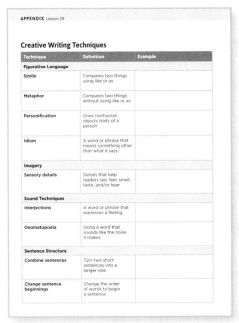

APPENDIX Lesson 19

Creative Writing Techniques

Technique	Definition	Example
Figurative Language		
Simile	Compares two things using *like* or *as*	
Metaphor	Compares two things without using *like* or *as*	
Personification	Gives nonhuman objects traits of a person	
Idiom	A word or phrase that means something other than what it says	
Imagery		
Sensory details	Details that help readers see, feel, smell, taste, and/or hear	
Sound Techniques		
Interjections	A word or phrase that expresses a feeling	
Onomatopoeia	Using a word that sounds like the noise it makes	
Sentence Structure		
Combine sentences	Turn two short sentences into a longer one	
Change sentence beginnings	Change the order of words to begin a sentence	

(See Appendix, page 142.)

31 "Humpty Dumpty" and "Little Boy Blue" are children's nursery rhymes that were written long ago. Nursery rhymes are simple stories that were often used to teach young children lessons. What is a lesson that "Humpty Dumpty" and "Little Boy Blue" teach children? How does each story teach that lesson? Use details from both stories to support your response.

In your response, be sure to:

- describe a lesson that both stories teach.
- explain how the lesson is taught in both stories.
- use details from both stories.

You may plan your writing for question 31 on the blank page provided (not shown).

Humpty Dumpty

Humpty Dumpty sat on a wall.
Humpty Dumpty had a great fall.
All the King's horses and all the King's men
Couldn't put Humpty Dumpty together again.

Little Boy Blue

Little Boy Blue, come blow your horn!
The sheep's in the meadow,
The cow's in the corn.
Where is that boy who looks after the sheep?
He's under a haystack, fast asleep.

"Humpty Dumpty" and "Little Boy Blue" are well-known children's nursery rhymes that were written centuries ago. Nursery rhymes are basic stories used to teach young children life lessons. Both of these teach a critical lesson easily and quickly.

A lesson both stories teach is that children should make smart choices. I know this because Humpty Dumpty makes a foolish choice by sitting on a wall. Little Boy Blue also makes a poor decision, choosing to sleep instead of work. **The choices both characters make are as big and bad as the Big Bad Wolf in "Little Red Riding Hood"!**

The lesson is taught in each story when the character's decision backfires **with a BOOM!** In "Humpty Dumpty," Humpty, an egg, foolishly sits on a wall. This is not so smart because next he has a "great fall" and breaks. Moreover, the evidence that follows shows that the King's horses and men "couldn't put Humpty back together again." In "Little Boy Blue," this lesson is taught when Little Boy Blue doesn't use good thinking and decides to sleep under a haystack instead of doing his job. First, he doesn't blow his horn to keep the sheep and cows from wandering away. In addition to this, people are looking for him and asking, "Where is the boy?" **Trouble will be waking him from his sleep!**

Children benefit from making smart choices is the lesson learned from these centuries-old nursery rhymes. This quick and easy lesson was good a long time ago and remains critical today.

(Available online.)

32 Scientists who study fish and mammals explain that they look the way they do often because their survival depends on it. In other words, these creatures may have special, easy-to-see features that help them survive in their environments. Write an essay that explains the features that some fish and mammals have that help them survive. Be sure to use facts and details from both passages to support your explanation.

Be sure to include:

• an introduction
• support for your ideas using information from the passages
• a conclusion that is relevant

Your response should be in the form of a multiple-paragraph essay. You may plan your writing for question 32 on the blank page provided (not shown).

Scientists help us understand that some fishes and mammals may have strange-looking features because their survival depends on it. After reading "When Looks Matter" and "It Came From the Mud," I learned about three creatures whose "ugly" features help them survive.

To begin, the pangolin is a mammal completely covered in scales. According to passage 1, it looks like it is wearing a coat of armor! **This medieval knight also uses its armor for battle.** It is covered from head to tail because it has to fend off predators. For example, tigers are one of its predators. The pangolin's armor keeps it safe against tigers' and other predators' sharp teeth.

In addition to the pangolin, the mudskipper has odd survival features. The mudskipper lives on land and in water (passage 2), so its special features help it survive in both environments. Its fins and tail help it move in the mud. It can even use its tail to jump. *Splosh, splosh, splosh . . . JUMP!* In addition, the mudskipper uses its gills to breathe. **The mudskipper didn't miss the boat when it comes to having all the right survival tools!**

Unlike the mudskipper, which uses its features to move and breathe, the seahorse is a creature with strange body parts that help it find food. As stated in passage 2, the seahorse can suck up tiny shrimp with its snout. Furthermore, it can grab onto plants with its tail. **The seahorse has everything it needs to enjoy every morsel of these tasty treats!**

Without question, scientists are right! These three creatures have special features that help them survive. The pangolin hinders predators with its coat of armor, the mudskipper easily survives on land and in water with its special body parts, and the seahorse uses its strange features to find food.

(Available online.)

Close-Up #2: When Looks Matter & It Came From the Mud

Display the sample response to question #32 (available online) on the board and hand out copies. Say to students: *Let's take a look at our extended response for "When Looks Matter" and "It Came From the Mud" and see what we can add.*

In the second paragraph, for example, we can add a metaphor, comparing the pangolin to a medieval knight. This metaphor works because the pangolin looks like it's wearing armor, like a knight. It also adds a detail that supports how it uses the armor—in battle. The next sentence better explains the kind of battle—protection against predators' sharp teeth.

Have students revisit the rest of the extended response and make some Add More & Explore revisions on their own. Encourage them to see where they may be able to combine two short sentences into one longer sentence or add onomatopoeia or an idiom or some imagery.

Allow students time to edit their extended response. Then discuss revisions they made and why.

Quick Close

Explain to students that the Add More & Explore strategy helps them move beyond structured response writing. It does this by helping them add techniques normally used in poetry and creative writing into their response writing:

• figurative language (simile, metaphor, personification, idiom)
• imagery (using sensory details)
• interjection and onomatopoeia (playful use of word sounds)
• sentence structure (combining sentences and changing sentence beginnings)

Caution students to use these techniques sparingly and skillfully to enrich their response writing.

Independent Readiness Survey

Gauge students' comfort level with using the Add More & Explore strategy in their responses. Read the numbered statements below and have students respond in one of three ways:

- Thumbs up if they agree
- Thumbs down if they disagree and want more guided practice with a teacher
- Thumbs midway if they almost agree but would like to work with a partner

1. I know how to use figurative language in my responses.
2. I know how to use imagery in my responses.
3. I know how to use word sounds to bring emotion into my responses.
4. I know how to use sentence techniques in my responses.

Teaching Notes

- All these Add More & Explore techniques are best introduced and practiced outside the Quick & Easy Lessons. For example, many teachers introduce creative writing techniques within a poetry unit and sentence techniques in a creative writing unit. Applying these techniques to response writing is the novelty.

- Determine beforehand which techniques students can easily insert as quick edits or revisions (such as interjections) and which ones you need to model during guided practice (such as sentence-structure techniques).

- Encourage students to try all of these techniques in their short and extended responses— but sparingly. Gauging when, where, and how to use them will take practice and modeling.

- You may wish to caution students about using too many techniques in a response. Suggesting one or two may help them strategically use a technique so it is effective. A just-right amount of technique enhances the quality of a response, while overuse can detract from its quality.

- Students should "control" the tone of their written responses. The techniques are fun, playful, and sometimes silly. Remind students that they should always be mindful of their tone, especially in tests.

- Help students recognize when their technique flows smoothly versus when it feels forced. This is especially true when using sensory details. The key is to carefully choose a sense that fits the context of the response. This will take some practice.

- A well-placed interjection or onomatopoeia can also add fun to a response. Both can add a playful glimmer of a writer's emotion.

LESSON 20 Develop Voice by Expanding Choice

Invite students to get to know the tone of their personal response-writing style.

Quick Start: You've learned to Stray & Play and to Add More & Explore. What's next in terms of developing your unique style? Develop Voice by Expanding Choice!

Making Connections

Say to students: *If your writing had a voice, what would it sound like? Voice is the unique sound of your writing. It is the way you share ideas with others in writing. It shows your personality, your attitude, and your style—and how you choose to use the strategies you've learned in these Quick & Easy Lessons. You choose how to express your good ideas. You choose what your response-writing voice will sound like.*

Display the "Response-Writing Voice Checklist" (page 143) on the board and discuss with the class.

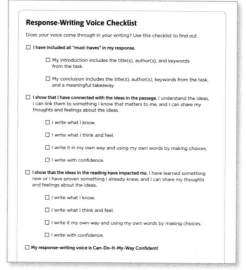

(See Appendix, page 143.)

Close-Up #1: Humpty Dumpty & Little Boy Blue

Display question #31 with revised response (available online) on the board. Say to students: *Let's take a look at how the writer added his voice to his response to the "Humpty Dumpty" and "Little Boy Blue" task from our earlier lessons. We'll see how this writer made various choices in his writing, and we'll listen to his response-writing voice.*

- In the introduction, the writer shows how he connects with the story by sharing his thoughts and feelings about nursery rhymes—as well as his knowledge of them. He includes all of the must-haves for an introduction (e.g., titles and keywords from the task) and brings his personality to his writing, as if he were writing in a response journal.

- The writer chooses to organize his ideas for two tasks—what the lesson was and how it was taught—into one paragraph.

- He also expresses his ideas about the lesson in his own way and using his own words: that children should make smart choices and be their own boss.

- The writer includes all RACE must-haves for the body paragraph. He includes his CRAFT techniques (from Lesson 17) and uses many of the creative techniques (from Lesson 19): he adds the onomatopoeia *SPLAT!* in all capital letters, and he uses different sentence structures.

- The writer includes all of the must-haves for a conclusion (e.g., titles, keywords, and takeaway), and he expresses the lesson in his own way and in his own words. He also shows a deeper-level connection to the lesson by adding: "Smart children should make smart choices." Additionally, he shows how the lesson impacted him and shares the advice he would give to his friends.

- In sum, his response has the sound and feel of an entry in a response-writing journal. His response-writing voice shows his personality, his attitude, and his style. It combines the must-haves with the Can-Do-It-My-Way Confidence!

31 "Humpty Dumpty" and "Little Boy Blue" are children's nursery rhymes that were written long ago. Nursery rhymes are simple stories that were often used to teach young children lessons. What is a lesson that "Humpty Dumpty" and "Little Boy Blue" teach children? How does each story teach that lesson? Use details from both stories to support your response.

In your response, be sure to:

- describe a lesson that both stories teach.
- explain how the lesson is taught in both stories.
- use details from both stories.

You may plan your writing for question 31 on the blank page provided (not shown).

Humpty Dumpty

Humpty Dumpty sat on a wall.
Humpty Dumpty had a great fall.
All the King's horses and all the King's men
Couldn't put Humpty Dumpty together again.

Little Boy Blue

Little Boy Blue, come blow your horn!
The sheep's in the meadow,
The cow's in the corn.
Where is that boy who looks after the sheep?
He's under a haystack, fast asleep.

Everyone knows the nursery rhymes "Humpty Dumpty" and "Little Boy Blue." Both have been around for centuries because they teach children critical life lessons. I liked rereading the nursery rhymes and thinking about the important lessons they teach!

Children should make good, smart choices! They should be their own boss! This is the lesson taught in each story. I know this because Humpty Dumpty makes a foolish choice by sitting on a wall. Little Boy Blue also makes a poor decision, choosing to sleep instead of work. The choices both characters make show they are not good bosses! Here's how the characters' choices backfire with a BOOM! In "Humpty Dumpty," Humpty, an egg, foolishly sits on a wall. This is not so smart because next he has a "great fall" and breaks. SPLAT! Moreover, the evidence that follows shows the King's horses and men "couldn't put Humpty back together again." Sadly, this isn't surprising! In "Little Boy Blue," this lesson is taught when Little Boy Blue doesn't use good thinking and decides to sleep under a haystack instead of doing his job. Not only does he let the sheep and cows wander away, but everyone is looking for him and asking, "Where is the boy?" Trouble will be waking him from his sleep!

Smart children should make smart choices is the lesson I learned from these centuries-old nursery rhymes. I would also add, "Be your own boss!" That's the advice I'd give my friends! This quick and easy lesson was good a long time ago and remains critical today, all thanks to Humpty Dumpty and Little Boy Blue.

(Available online.)

Close-Up #2: When Looks Matter & It Came From the Mud

Display question #32 with revised response (available online) on the board and say: *Now, let's take a look at this response to the "When Looks Matter" and "It Came from the Mud" task from our earlier lessons.*

- In the introduction, the writer shows she connects with the story by sharing her good-humored thinking that survival sometimes depends on ugly or unusual features. We also sense her feelings through her words "great new facts." She makes it clear that she enjoys learning new ideas from this article. She also includes all of the must-haves for an introduction (e.g., titles and keywords from the task) and shows her personality through her writing.

- The writer chooses to organize her ideas into separate paragraphs and gives references to the passages. She also includes a lot of evidence from the text, using different transitions every time. This helps her meet the must-have requirements and also nicely balances the number of her own thoughts and feelings.

- The writer includes all of the must-haves for a conclusion, and she expresses her understanding in her own way and in her own words.

32 Scientists who study fish and mammals explain that they look the way they do often because their survival depends on it. In other words, these creatures may have special, easy-to-see features that help them survive in their environments. Write an essay that explains the features that some fish and mammals have that help them survive. Be sure to use facts and details from both passages to support your explanation.

Be sure to include:

- an introduction
- support for your ideas using information from the passages
- a conclusion that is relevant

Your response should be in the form of a multiple-paragraph essay. You may plan your writing for question 32 on the blank page provided (not shown).

Survival can get ugly! What I mean is best described by scientists who help us understand that fish and mammals may have strange-looking—downright "ugly" or unusual—features because their survival depends on it. After reading "When Looks Matter" and "It Came From the Mud," I learned great new facts about three creatures whose "ugly" features help them survive.

To begin, the pangolin is a mammal completely covered in scales. According to passage 1, it looks like it is wearing a coat of armor! Even though the pangolin doesn't have the warrior look of a medieval knight, its scales are useful for predator protection. As stated in the article, the pangolin's scales can keep it safe against tigers' or other predators' sharp teeth. After successfully fending off predators like tigers, the pangolin is probably very thankful for its weird scales.

In addition to the pangolin, the mudskipper has odd-looking survival features. The mudskipper lives on land and in water (passage 2), so its special features help it survive in both environments. Its fins and tail help it move in the mud, and it can even use its tail to jump! That must be funny to see and probably explains how the mudskipper got its name. In addition, the article informs us that the mudskipper uses its gills to breathe. The mudskipper didn't miss the boat when it comes to having all the right survival tools!

Unlike the mudskipper which uses its features to move and breathe, the seahorse is a creature with really cool body parts that help it find food. As stated in passage 2, the seahorse can suck up tiny shrimp with its snout. Furthermore, it can grab onto plants with its tail. Although these features don't make the seahorse ugly, they are peculiar looking. It's easy to see how a seahorse is like a horse grazing, only at the bottom of the ocean instead of in a field.

There are benefits to ugly and unusual. Without question, scientists are right! These three creatures have special features that help them survive. The pangolin hinders predators with its coat of armor, the mudskipper easily survives on land and in water with its special body parts, and the seahorse uses its strange features to find food. Understanding the reasons behind ugly and unusual is a beautiful lesson to learn!

(Available online.)

- She also shows a deep level of connection to the lesson throughout her response. She shares her thoughts on the mudskipper's name and how the seahorse is like other horses.

- We also see that the information in the article has impacted her based on her last sentence: "Understanding the reasons behind ugly and unusual is a beautiful lesson to learn!" She also ends as she began, with a just-right amount of humor.

Encourage students to go back to their extended response and look for ways to add their voice to their writing.

Quick Close

Say to students: *The Develop Voice by Expanding Choice strategy helps us move beyond structured response writing because we can choose the best way to express our ideas. It shows us how to use our response-writing voice, which combines our personality, attitude, style, AND the strategies we've learned in our Quick & Easy Lessons! We choose how to use them. We choose how to express our good ideas and what our response-writing voice will sound like.*

Independent Readiness Survey

Gauge students' comfort level with adding voice to their responses. Read the numbered statements below and have students respond in one of three ways:

- Thumbs up if they agree
- Thumbs down if they disagree and want more guided practice with a teacher
- Thumbs midway if they almost agree but would like to work with a partner

1. I know how to include the must-haves in my responses.
2. I know I can write what I know and what I think and feel in my responses.
3. I know I can write in my own words and in my own way, as I choose, in my responses.
4. My response-writing voice is Can-Do-It-My-Way Confident!

Teaching Notes

- Read aloud the responses to Close-Up #1 and #2 so students can listen for voice. Helping students hear how voice sounds in an exemplar passage may help them recognize voice in their own writing.

- You may wish to set gentle parameters for the overall tone of students' written responses. The tone of a strong, well-written response is best described as "formal yet friendly," and students may need guidance understanding this.

- Helping students find their "response-writing voice" may take coaxing for some students (those who struggle to engage) and steering for other (those who push the limits of a formal yet friendly tone). Provide differentiated feedback to all students on their practice responses.

- Make sure students have effectively addressed all of the must-haves (for short and/or extended responses) in their writing. Their authentic response-writing voice will solidly enrich a strong answer, but it will not compensate for a weak one.

- A student's unique response-writing voice can sparkle as the result of as few as one or two stand-out literary moments; this could be through vocabulary, transitions, the originality of their views, and so on. Encourage students to try out many different ways to express an idea, while also reminding them that overuse can take away from a response.

- Provide students with routine opportunities to respond authentically to fiction and nonfiction texts to help them build an authentic response-writing voice. This activity is easy to integrate into classroom instruction, including content-area instruction.

Appendix

BE A SUPER READER!

How does a SUPER READER use his superpowers?

X-RAY VISION

to see through a piece of text and find...

☆ **main idea**
☆ **theme**
☆ **characters**
☆ **setting**
☆ **problem and solution**
☆ **and more**

MANIPULATE TIME

to slow down or speed up reading—to reread, retell, or summarize—and know when to do each one

POWERS OF PREDICTION

to identify whether the text is fact or fiction — and plan how to "attack" the text

What's in a Super Reader's UTILITY BELT?

Text-Marking Strategies, such as:

☆ **underlining**
☆ **codes and symbols**
☆ **gist statements**
☆ **hashtags**

BE A SUPER WRITER!

How does a SUPER WRITER tackle writing tasks?

Uses **QUESTION-ATTACK** strategies to **blast through** a question to uncover what it's really asking

Shape-shift or edit writing by using **CUPS**.

C apitalization

U sage and understanding

P unctuation

S pelling

No need for **super speed** when you can **RACE!**

R estate the question

A nswer

C ite evidence/details

E dit or explain

DRAWS UPON STAMINA OF STEEL
to write short and extended answers

The Star-Spangled Banner

by Francis Scott Key

O say can you see, by the dawn's early light,

What so proudly we hail'd at the twilight's last gleaming,

Whose broad stripes and bright stars through the perilous fight

O'er the ramparts we watch'd were so gallantly streaming?

And the rocket's red glare, the bombs bursting in air,

Gave proof through the night that our flag was still there,

O say does that star-spangled banner yet wave

O'er the land of the free and the home of the brave?

Take Action Close-Reading Strategies Checklist

☐ **1.** Slow down

☐ **2.** Reread

☐ **3.** Stay focused

☐ **4.** Read punctuation

☐ **5.** Pause and think

☐ **6.** Read aloud when needed (during silent reading)

☐ **7.** Pause and summarize

☐ **8.** Pause and restate in your own words

☐ **9.** Pause and rest

☐ **10.** Track lines/words/paragraphs

I can, you can, we can read . . . in a Close-Reading Way!

Picnic Tricks

by Jack Sprat

"We're going to have the best picnic ever!" Tina called. She added grapes to a bright yellow lunch bag.

"Aw, Tina. Picnics are no fun," said Scooter. He leaned against the screen door. "Ants always sneak onto my sandwich. Sometimes I eat them by mistake!" He scowled. "They taste yucky."

Tina stepped out to the porch, pulling the strap of the lunch bag over her shoulder. The door banged closed behind her.

"Doesn't have to be that way, Scooter," she said. She helped him off the porch and led the way to the backyard. "Always look for ants before taking a bite. If you see any, use the Flick Trick, like this." She ran her pointer finger quickly across the bottom of her thumb, pretending to flick an ant off her arm. "That's my trick for getting rid of pests on a picnic."

"Thanks, Tina," he said, stopping to test his flicking skills. He thought it was a good trick.

"I'd like to picnic near the ferns," Tina said, pointing to the part of her yard that butted up to Mrs. Major's house.

Scooter stopped in his tracks. "Aw, Tina. Not there! Zippy lives in the house by the ferns! When I play in my sandbox, he runs over and jumps on me. He licks my face all over." He cringed.

"Doesn't have to be that way, Scooter," Tina said, waving for him to catch up. "If Zippy visits our picnic, do the Scratch Trick." Tina hooked her thumbs together, spread her fingers and curled them slightly. "Bend down and give Zippy a good scratch behind his ears." She wiggled her fingers as if scratching. "That's my trick for keeping a jumpy puppy down on a picnic."

"Thanks, Tina," Scooter said, twisting his fingers into shape. He thought it was a good trick.

When they reached the fern bed, Tina found a perfect clearing. No sooner had she set the lunch bag down when — "Yap! Yap! Yap-pity, Yap!" — a frisky puppy sped toward them.

"Aw, Tina . . . It's ZIPPY!"

In a flash, Scooter had his doggy scratcher in place like a shield, but the frisky puppy lurched toward the lunch bag instead. He grabbed the strap and ran off.

"Stop, Zippy!" cried Tina, trailing after the thief. Sandwiches, grapes, and other treats flew from the lunch bag, which had come open in the commotion.

Scooter watched as Zippy led Tina on a high-speed chase until finally, the tired pooch dropped the emptied lunch bag and jogged home.

"Aw, Scooter," Tina said. "The puppy has made a mess of our lunch!" She scooped up some squished grapes and dropped them into the soiled lunch bag. "Our best picnic ever is in shambles."

Scooter wasn't used to seeing his friend without a fix-it trick . . . but perhaps it was now his turn.

"Aw, Tina, it doesn't have to be that way!" As Tina hunted through the ferns to clean up, Scooter ran back to his house and returned in no time. He was carrying a brown paper bag.

"One PBJ for you, and one PBJ for me." He handed Tina a sandwich. "Do-Overs!" he said. "That's my trick for fixing picnics." He flicked off an ant that had snuck onto his sandwich and smiled at Tina.

"Do-Overs!" she cheered. "That's the best trick ever!"

They each took a big bite of sandwich.

When Looks Matter

Pangolins live in Africa and Asia.

Which animal would you rather snuggle up with—a panda cub or a blobfish? Most people would say the panda, but not scientist Lucy Cooke. She takes pictures and videos of the world's oddest-looking creatures. She wants to teach people about these animals before it's too late. Many, like the proboscis monkey, are endangered and could use a helping hand.

Animal Planet

There are more than 10,000 known **endangered** animal species in the world. But a recent study found that groups that protect animals usually focus on cute, cuddly creatures. Why? It's easier to convince people to help them. That's bad news for the ugly animals—and for the animals and plants around them.

Words to Know

endangered: in danger of dying out

ecosystem: a group of animals and plants that live together

predators: animals that eat other animals

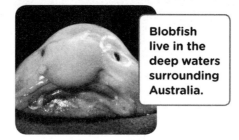

Blobfish live in the deep waters surrounding Australia.

When a species dies out, its entire **ecosystem** can be harmed.

Every animal plays an important role in an ecosystem. Take frogs, for example. Yes, they can be slimy. But if they were to disappear, the snakes and birds that eat them could die out too. And with no frogs to gobble up bugs, the number of insects might get out of control.

Ugly for a Reason

Cooke says there's a good reason that animals aren't all adorable. Often the things we find weird in animals help them survive in the wild. She points to one of her favorite animals—the pangolin.

The pangolin is covered from head to tail with large, hard scales. This body armor protects it from toothy **predators** like tigers.

Cooke hopes that her work will make people care about all animals, no matter what they look like.

"Once you understand why they're ugly or odd," she says, "I hope you'll appreciate and want to save them as much as I do."

Proboscis (pruh-BAH-sis) monkeys live in Borneo, an island nation in Asia.

Deep in the Ocean

by Jack Sprat

"What were once called fearsome sea monsters—with thick arms, huge, unblinking eyes, and a bird-like beak—are nowadays known as giant squid. But in many ways, despite scientific advances, they remain a mystery."

As Karen began reading an informational article on giant squid, she felt the hair on the back of her neck stand up. She stopped reading and placed her tablet beside her on the beach blanket.

"Can we go in now?" shouted her little sister, Jessie. Jessie was near the water, splashing in the shallow tide that rolled onto the sand.

"Not yet," Karen shouted a quick reply as she shifted her position in her beach chair. She glanced out to the ocean and cringed.

"C'mon, please? Mom said I can't go in unless you're with me." Jessie braced her feet firmly in the sand. As the tide retreated, she pleaded again, "Please? Oh pretty please, Karen?"

"I'll be ready in a few more minutes." Karen picked up her tablet and returned to the article. She thought maybe the squid might be confined to the Atlantic Ocean. She and her family vacationed in California and enjoyed the beaches along the Pacific coast. She reached for her tablet and scanned the article.

"Scientists believe that giant squid inhabit the Atlantic and the Pacific Oceans. This is based on remains found in whales that were captured or washed up on both coastal beaches."

Karen sighed as she put her tablet back down. Again she looked out to the vast ocean and shivered.

"C'mon, Karen. It's been a few more minutes." Jessie motioned for her sister to join her with an impatient wave.

"Just a few more minutes," Karen replied.

Jessie ran to the blanket and flopped down next to her sister. "I'll wait here until you're ready," she said, pouting. She grabbed the tablet, which opened to the article Karen had been reading. "Hey look, here's an article on those giant squid. Good thing we'll never see them in the ocean," Jessie laughed.

"What makes you so sure?" asked Karen.

"On our field trip to the Aquarium last week, Director James said the squid stay in the deep, deep, deepest part of the oceans. That's why scientists haven't ever seen them. He said we'd more likely see a real-life mermaid than a giant squid!"

Karen and Jessie laughed.

"I think it's time to go look for mermaids," said Karen, chuckling. She rose from her beach chair and began running toward the water. "Come on, Jessie, I'll race you," she hollered.

Teacher Notes

This passage has mixed clues. Some may think it is fiction based on the illustration and brief paragraphs, which suggest an exchange of character dialogue. Also, there is an absence of headings and other informational features, such as glossary or sidebars.

However, some may think it is informational based on the unusual italicized and quoted text at the beginning.

While mixed clues may cause reader uncertainty, a good discussion about "testing" your Jump-Start ideas is a great lesson. Helping students apply their literary skill—yet knowing they have to test them out—is valuable. In the Jump-Start stage, using the scanning process—setting flexible expectations that are based on their growing literary knowledge, knowing they can change their expectations—is more important than being "correct" before they've read the passage.

Ask Joan the Bone Hunter

Dear Joan,

I want to be an **archaeologist**. I've known this since kindergarten . . . three years ago! Back then, I didn't know an arch from an archaeologist! Even Zeb, my pet mudpuppy, couldn't believe there was a special name for scientists who like digging up things. I've found tons of old things buried in the woods behind my house— even animal bones! I wanna be an archaeologist. Can you help us learn more about archaeologists?

Your friends,
Bennie & Zeb,
Dirt-Diggers & Lovers of Bones
and All Buried Things!

Hey there, Bennie and Zeb!

When I read your letter, I couldn't wait to tell you about Drs. Holley and Jackie. Both are archaeologists. They study very different things.

Dr. Holley Moyes studies really old pottery, like clay pots. She examines them closely. She even looks for finger markings that show if pieces were pinched into shape. "We look at everything— the shape of the pot, its size, if there are handles." Dr. Holley tries to uncover how the pottery was made. She uses those clues to help her date when the piece was made.

Like you, Bennie, Dr. Holley showed an early interest in archaeology. Here's her story:

"When I was in kindergarten, I invited my friends to go on a 'dig' in our sand pile. I buried all of my plastic dinosaurs there. Everyone loved digging them up! I also remember family trips. We'd pass a sign for a cave, and I thought that was the most wonderful thing ever. I begged my parents to stop!"

It seems Dr. Holley enjoyed playful backyard digs, too. She also enjoyed family trips to caves.

Dr. Jackie Eng is a **bioarchaeologist**. She studies very old human bones. From this, Dr. Jackie learns more about people who lived long ago. "Being able to explore people in the past and giving a voice to them and their lived experience is a highlight of what I do." Dr. Jackie works at **dig sites** with many other scientists. She sets up a **field laboratory** where she photographs and records notes about bones that are found there. Using special tools, Dr. Jackie can uncover a lot of facts about the bones. For example, she can tell if a bone belonged to a male or female.

Here's a great story Dr. Jackie shares about how she became interested in archaeology:

"I was a kid with many unusual interests. While I enjoyed school, I couldn't find anything that matched all of my interests—until I saw a picture of 'Lucy.' She's the famous first early human. Right then, I knew that biological anthropology was the field for me!"

It seems Dr. Jackie likes to study bones like you do, Bennie. She even studies collections kept in museums. Why not visit a museum?

So, Benny & Zeb, I hope these ideas help you chase your interests. Drs. Holley and Jackie send a huge "Happy Digging" shout out!

Till next time,
Joan

Dr. Holley Moyes

Dr. Jackie Eng

Teacher Notes

Is this fact or fiction? This passage has mixed features—an avatar and real-life photographs. Vocabulary words are bold, and the format is not typical for fact or fiction. It appears to be a letter requesting help. Maybe it's fiction, and Bennie and Zeb are characters. The problem is they need help to learn about archaeologists. But then again, it could be fact—especially since Drs. Holley and Jackie are real archaeologists. The passage talks about what Dr. Holley does and how she got started. The quotation marks indicate those are Dr. Holley's actual words. It also tells about Dr. Jackie in the same way.

Could this passage be both fact and fiction? It seems this passage uses both fact and fiction to help make learning about archaeology fun. From this passage, we learn that there are different kinds of archaeologists. Also, there's a lot of things we can do now to learn more about archaeology.

Jamel's Visit

Jamel had been at Great Grandpa Charles's home for only thirty minutes when he tucked his chin in his hands and let out a big sigh. He wished he had brought his iPad from home. He had some great new games he could play, if only his mother hadn't discouraged him from bringing it along. Jamel couldn't believe his mom had to leave him at his great grandfather's house all morning. She had to run several errands and didn't want Jamel to be alone in their apartment.

Jamel glanced around his great grandfather's small living room for the tenth time. It all pretty much looked the same as the last nine times, until he suddenly spied a picture hanging on the wall. In it, a man in uniform was standing in front of an airplane. Jamel hadn't noticed the picture before.

"I see you've found my new picture," Great Grandpa Charles said as he entered the room with a plate of cookies and some milk. "Bet you can't guess who's in it?"

Although Jamel hoped his great grandfather wouldn't try to play a silly guessing game, at least the time might pass a little faster.

"I think it's you, when you were younger?" guessed Jamel. "Is it from the war?" Jamel knew his great grandfather had been in a war, but he tuned out pretty quickly whenever his great grandfather's war stories began. Jamel meant no disrespect, he just couldn't grasp a lot of what happened way back then.

"Pretty good guess!" said his great grandfather. "Indeed, it is me when I flew as a Tuskegee Airman. We were the first African American military group to fly in World War II."

Jamel suddenly jumped to his feet, rushed to the wall, and peered closely at the photograph. He had been learning about the Tuskegee Airmen in school. His teacher, Ms. Taylor, had shown a movie about them and explained how hard it was for them to be treated respectfully, with equality.

"For real? You were a Tuskegee Airman?" gasped Jamel. "Tell me all about it," he begged.

Great Grandpa Charles handed Jamel the plate of cookies and a glass of milk and began. "When I was much younger . . ."

A Fan Named Fanny

An Unlikely Friend to President Abraham Lincoln

by Frédérique D'Amour

Abraham Lincoln (left)
Fanny Seward (right)

If you cheer "Hooray! Ya-hoo! Whoopee!" and do The Wave when your favorite sports team scores, then you're a fan. If you clap your hands and rock-out with some cool moves when your favorite celeb performs on stage, then you're a fan, too.

It's not surprising that most kids are fans of something—singers, actors, athletes—even presidents! Abraham Lincoln, the 13th president of the United States, is a HUGE favorite.

But what is surprising is that a long time ago, a very special young girl named Frances Adeline Seward, "Fanny" for short, was a most unlikely fan of President Lincoln. "Unlikely" because her father, William Henry Seward, was supposed to be president instead. At least that's what Fanny thought!

Fanny's dad and Mr. Lincoln were "rivals." This term describes people who compete for the same thing. Although both men wanted to become president, Seward lost an election for president to Lincoln. This ended his chances of running for president.

To make matters worse, Seward's loss was a BIG surprise. Fanny, and nearly everyone else who lived in

Auburn, New York, was sure he would win. They even started their victory party early! There were many sad faces, Fanny's among them, when the votes were counted and the winner—Mr. Abraham Lincoln—was announced.

So, why would Fanny be a fan of the man who beat out her father to the U.S. presidency? The notes Fanny left behind in her miniature-size diaries might give us some clues.

It could be because when Fanny and her father visited President Lincoln in his Washington, D.C., home—the White House—the president's welcome was warm and friendly. Fanny couldn't help but like him right away.

"I liked him very much," Fanny wrote in September 1861. "He received us very cordially."

It also might be because President Lincoln was very "fond" of kittens. Fanny wrote in her diary that Lincoln showed them his "pretty" kittens, which were playing inside the home. He says "they climb all over him," she added. Fanny was an animal lover—apparently just like President Lincoln!

Thanks to her diaries, Fanny helped us puzzle together little-known pieces of history and consider new ideas about people, places, and events. Here, she showed us that although an unlikely fan, she was, in fact, very much a fan of President Abraham Lincoln—"Hooray! Ya-hoo! Whoopee!"

Think & Discuss: Advanced I Spy for Fiction/Literature

What's on the page?

- I spy _pictures_, so I think _this is a story_.
- I spy _many short paragraphs of dialogue (use of quotation marks)_, so I think _this is a story_.

- I spy _____ in the title, so I think this is a story about _____.
- Other ideas: _____

Think & Discuss: Advanced I Spy for Nonfiction/Informational Text

What's on the page?

- I spy _photographs_, so I think _this is an article_.
- I spy _subheadings_, so I think _this is an article_.
- I spy _____ in the title, so I think this is an article about _____ .
- Other ideas: _____

Think & Discuss: What I Know About...

Most Stories	Most Articles
I know . . . • in the beginning, a character has a problem. • in the middle, the character tries to solve it through events. • in the end, there is a solution. • the character learns something new. • the reader learns a life lesson.	I know . . . • an author wants to inform us about a topic through text and possibly visuals. • the author shares key ideas about the topic in paragraphs. • each paragraph has details. • there are many kinds of details and many ways to tell about them. • the author makes an overall point (main idea) about the topic. • the reader learns information.

Steps for Underlining and Coding a Story/Literature

☐ 1. Read the title. Underline clues about the story elements.

☐ 2. Number the paragraphs for the whole story.

☐ 3. Read the paragraphs slowly, using your pencil to track the words.

☐ 4. As you read, select key elements to underline—characters, setting, problem(s), key events, and the solution. You may wish to pause after a major event or an important exchange of dialogue and reread to be sure you've underlined key elements.

☐ 5. Simultaneously code the elements in the margin using a simple system.

C = characters

S = setting

P = problem

E = event

Sol = solution

Steps for Underlining and Coding Informational Text

☐ 1. Read the title. Underline clues about the topic.

☐ 2. Number the paragraphs for the whole article.

☐ 3. Read paragraph 1, using your pencil to track the words.

☐ 4. Reread paragraph 1 and select key ideas to underline. As a guide, underline only key ideas that would help you present an oral summary of the paragraph.

☐ 5. Repeat this for each paragraph.

☐ 6. You may detect the main idea expressed in a sentence at the beginning, the end, or in the middle of the paragraph. Code it in the margin using a simple *MI*.

Text-Marking Add-Ons

We read with our pencils!

Circle words = (unknown, interesting vocabulary words)

Underline = important ideas

Box ideas = dates, numbers

Reactions to text and inner voice

? = wonderings, questions, don't understand

! = excitement, surprise

☺ ☹ = emotions/feelings
while you read

1, 2, 3 = number paragraphs,
lists, and ideas

Lesson 6 Close-Up #1

Picnic Tricks
by Jack Sprat

S

1 "We're going to have the best picnic ever!"
☺ C Tina called. She added grapes to a bright yellow
lunch bag.

2 "Aw, Tina. Picnics are no fun," said Scooter.
He leaned against the screen door. "Ants always
☹ P sneak onto my sandwich. Sometimes I eat them by
mistake!" He (scowled.) "They taste yucky."

3 Tina stepped out to the porch, pulling the strap
of the lunch bag over her shoulder. The door banged
closed behind her.

4 "Doesn't have to be that way, Scooter," she said.
She helped him off the porch and led the way to
the backyard. "Always look for ants before taking a
E1 bite. If you see any, use the Flick Trick, like this." She
! ran her pointer finger quickly across the bottom of
her thumb, pretending to flick an ant off her arm.
"That's my trick for getting rid of pests on a picnic."

5 "Thanks, Tina," he said, stopping to test his flicking
skills. He thought it was a good trick.

6 "I'd like to picnic near the ferns," Tina said,
pointing to the part of her yard that butted up to
Mrs. Major's house.

7 C Scooter stopped in his tracks. "Aw, Tina. Not there!
Zippy lives in the house by the ferns! When I play in
my sandbox, he runs over and jumps on me. He licks
P my face all over." He (cringed.)

☹ 8 "Doesn't have to be that way, Scooter," Tina said,
waving for him to catch up. "If Zippy visits our picnic,
E2 do the Scratch Trick." Tina hooked her thumbs
together, spread her fingers and curled them slightly.
"Bend down and give Zippy a good scratch behind
his ears." She wiggled her fingers as if scratching.
! "That's my trick for keeping a jumpy puppy down
on a picnic."

9 "Thanks, Tina," Scooter said, twisting his fingers
into shape. He thought it was a good trick.

10 When they reached the fern bed, Tina found
a perfect clearing. No sooner had she set the lunch

bag down when — "Yap! Yap! Yap-pity, Yap!" —
a frisky puppy sped toward them.

11 "Aw, Tina . . . It's ZIPPY!" P

12 In a flash, Scooter had his doggy scratcher
in place like a shield, but the frisky puppy (lurched)
toward the lunch bag instead. He grabbed the strap
and ran off.

13 "Stop, Zippy!" cried Tina, trailing after the thief. ☹
Sandwiches, grapes, and other treats flew from the P
lunch bag, which had come open in the commotion.

14 Scooter watched as Zippy led Tina on a high-
speed chase until finally, the tired pooch dropped
the emptied lunch bag and jogged home.

15 "Aw, Scooter," Tina said. "The puppy has made a P
mess of our lunch!" She scooped up some squished
grapes and dropped them into the (soiled) lunch bag.
"Our best picnic ever is in (shambles.")

16 Scooter wasn't used to seeing his friend without
a fix-it trick . . . but perhaps it was now his turn.

17 "Aw, Tina, it doesn't have to be that way!" As Tina ?
hunted through the ferns to clean up, Scooter ran
back to his house and returned in no time. He was
carrying a brown paper bag.

18 "One PBJ for you, and one PBJ for me."
He handed Tina a sandwich. "Do-Overs!" he said. E3
"That's my trick for fixing picnics." He flicked off an !
ant that had snuck onto his sandwich and smiled at
Tina.

19 "Do-Overs!" she cheered. "That's the best trick Sol
ever!" ☺

20 They each took a big bite of sandwich.

Humpty Dumpty

Humpty Dumpty sat on a wall.
Humpty Dumpty had a great fall.
All the King's horses and all the King's men
Couldn't put Humpty Dumpty together again.

1 What happened to Humpty Dumpty?
Use two details to support your response.

_____

_____

_____

_____

_____

2 At the beginning of the nursery rhyme, Humpty Dumpty decides to sit on a wall.
Why was this decision unwise? Use two details from the story to support your answer.

_____

_____

_____

_____

_____

An Extreme Adventure
by Frédérique D'Amour

Bungee jumping! Snowboarding! Zip lining! Just thinking about these extreme sports sets our goose bumps hoppin'! Dizzying speeds, harrowing heights, grueling demands, and DANGER have earned these sports respect, not to mention WOW-appeal!

Yet, *what's next?* is the question every extremist asks. If it's got to push the limits, challenge human skill, and pose danger, Alex Aquilino could be the athlete to champion the cause. He's not a bungee jumper, nor a snowboarder, nor even a zip liner. Alex is a dancer—a special kind of dancer called a "swing."

"A swing's job is to fill in for members of an ensemble (cast of dancers) at a moment's notice," explains Alex. "If anyone becomes ill, injured, or can't perform because of an emergency, I cover for them."

As a swing for a popular Broadway musical, Alex is ready to take the stage to perform in place of other male cast members—not one, not two, but FIVE in all! This means he must learn the dancers' routines and be prepared to slip on stage and perform flawlessly for all of them.

"It's a little stressful, but it never becomes stale," Alex says with a laugh. "There are a lot of small movements, facial gestures, and other subtle touches that go along with the different and often difficult dance routines. The way you hold a prop matters a lot. Getting everything right is challenging."

In order to perfect his performances, Alex works tirelessly with the show's dance captain to master the choreography, which is a type of script for the dance routines. Alex knows that he must perform all five routines with precision and artistry. The demands on his strength, agility, and stamina must parallel, if not surpass, that of many extreme athletes!

"I started by learning one person's track (routines), and after I got a handle on that, then I'd learn the next person's," Alex said. "I also had to learn their backstage movements."

Not surprisingly, Alex had to mimic how the dancers exited the stage, where they went, how they prepared for their next routine, and their pace and timing. "The smallest details were critical." Sometimes, Alex's entire day was spent following dancers backstage.

"Becoming a swing takes a unique skill set. You have to have talent, but there's also a brainpower swings have. They must be dedicated to perfection."

There's no doubt that Alex is dedicated to perfection. It is also certain that he and other dance swings push the limits and challenge human ability. Yet, does dancing pose the same dangers as extreme sports? Some statistics show that 43 percent of dancers between the ages of 10 to 18 sustain injuries. For professional dancers like Alex, this number increases from 67 to 95 percent. Ouch!

It seems swings like Alex perform just like other extreme athletes; they face similar challenges . . . and even dangers.

Zorbing, Powerblocking, Blobbing, and XPogo-ing may hope to top the "Newbie" list of extremes. Yet dancing with the heart, soul, and grit of a swing may truly be the Supreme of Extremes!

1 What main idea is supported in paragraph 6 of "An Extreme Adventure"? Use two details to support your response.

_____

_____

_____

_____

_____

_____

2 Why is paragraph 1 of "An Extreme Adventure" an effective introduction? Use two details to support your answer.

_____

_____

_____

_____

_____

_____

3 In "An Extreme Adventure," what do paragraphs 4 and 5 show us about Alex? Use two details to support your answer.

_____

_____

_____

_____

_____

_____

Question-Attack Strategies Checklist

☐ **1.** To locate the question, circle the question mark and trace backward to the beginning of the question. Some short-response questions are long. They begin with a sentence about the passage and end with a direction, such as: *Use two details from the passage to support your answer.* The question falls in between the two statements. Find the question mark, and you'll find the question!

☐ **2.** Box the *who, what*, *when*, *where*, *why*, or *how* word at the beginning of the question. This is a clue about what information to include in an answer.

☐ **3.** Based on the clue in the question (#2 above), think about some ways to answer.

When this CLUE is in the question . . .	. . . my ANSWER should include . . .
Who	main or minor characters, people, groups, or others listed in the passage
What	objects, thoughts, feelings, words, ideas, actions, events
When	time, events
Where	place, physical location, setting
Why	*because . . .*
How	*by . . ., because . . .*

☐ **4.** Underline key or important words, such as the subject (who or what) and the verb (action) so the question is clear.

☐ **5.** Box locations, such as lines, paragraphs, or sections, that are stated in a question.

☐ **6.** Look for the words *explain*, *describe*, or *discuss*, and think about some ways to answer.

When this ACTION word is in the question . . .	. . . my ANSWER should. . .
Explain	make something understandable, give reasons or causes, show connections
Describe	tell about something using sensory details
Discuss	share facts, reasons, and details to make a point

Restating the Question Checklist

When it comes to restating the question, there are three levels of skill building. These levels are based on the kinds of changes you may need to do to construct a smooth-sounding beginning. Whisper-read your writing as you start your response to help you make decisions about how to restate the question.

☐ **Simple** Nothing needs to be done to make the restated section flow smoothly.

☐ **Average** Only a few changes are needed to make the restated section flow smoothly. Changes could include:

- streamlining and omitting part of the question.

- swapping words in the question to make the meaning clear.

- reworking a clumsy-sounding sentence.

☐ **Challenging** A lot of shaping and restructuring is needed to make the restated sentence flow smoothly. You may have to:

- restructure several areas of the question.

- use two or more sentences to express complex ideas.

- use words from the question in other ways, such as at the end of your answer instead of at the beginning.

Think & Discuss: Ingredients of an Inference

- **A sprinkle of background knowledge.** We experience and understand many of the same things as our classmates and friends. We use this shared know-how when we read. Sometimes authors don't need to tell us everything.

- **A dash of reading between and beyond the lines.** We can also piece together our understanding from things we learn elsewhere in a story or a passage. Sometimes authors don't tell us everything but give us clues.

- **A pinch of text evidence.** Even though we can use our background knowledge and read between and beyond the lines, we still must support our ideas with solid text evidence.

Little Boy Blue

Little Boy Blue, come blow your horn!
The sheep's in the meadow,
The cow's in the corn.
Where is that boy who looks after the sheep?
He's under a haystack, fast asleep.

1 What does the passage tell us about Little Boy Blue?
Use two details to support your answer.

_____

_____

_____

_____

_____

_____

_____

_____

_____

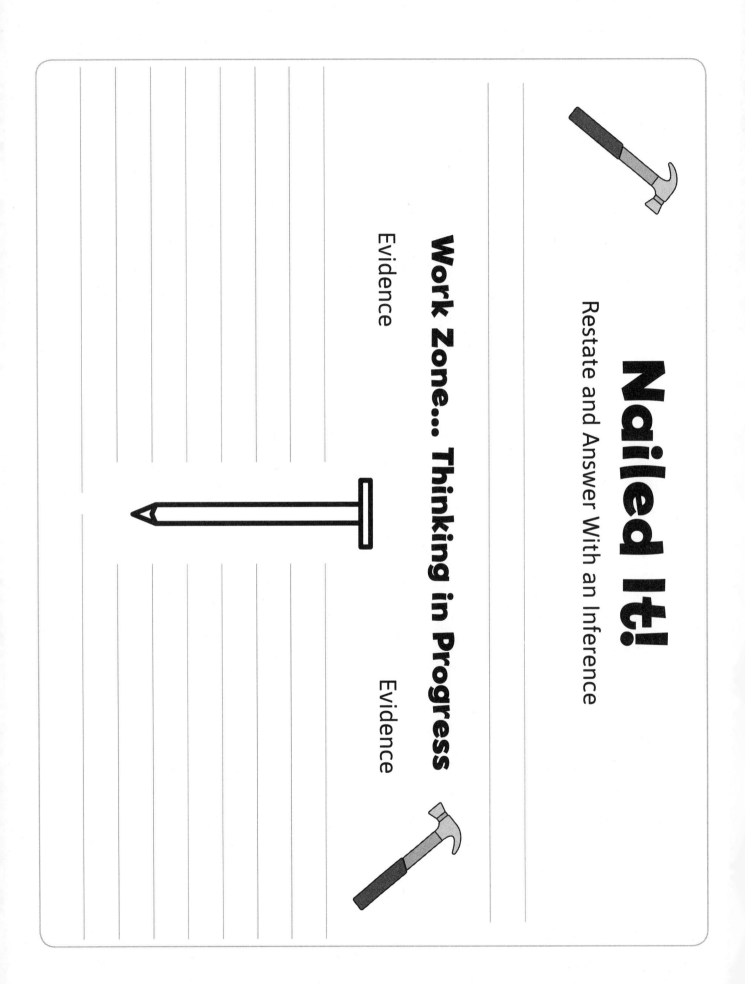

Nailed It!
Restate and Answer With an Inference

Work Zone... Thinking in Progress

Evidence

Evidence

Think-It-Through Inferencing Strategies

- **Bottom-Up Strategy** Sometimes we have to carefully think through the evidence first. Then come up with an inference that squares with the evidence.

- **Top-Down Strategy** Other times we seem to "just know" something (in other words, we quickly infer something), but we still have to use evidence to explain how we know.

Both strategies work!

Helpful Tools for Making Inferences

- **Nailed It! graphic organizer** This organizer works with both strategies. For the Bottom-Up Strategy, fill in the evidence area first and then make an inference. For the Top-Down Strategy, fill in the inference first, then find evidence to support your idea.

- **Think-It-Through planning grid** This is just like a Nailed It! graphic organizer, but you can quickly draw it on your own. You can explain (E) the details you've chosen, too.

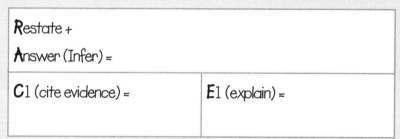

Restate + Answer (Infer) =	
C1 (cite evidence) =	E1 (explain) =

- **"From this, I can infer . . ." statement** Using the RA + C + E letters in the margin (or embedded in the answer) reminds us to "Restate and Answer" with our inference. We can also put it in the end using the "infer statement."

---

44 In "Excerpt from *Hattie Big Sky*," what do paragraphs 18 and 19 show about Hattie? Use two details from the story to support your answer.

(RA)   Paragraphs 18 and 19 show many things about Hattie. In paragraph 18,

(C1)   Hattie "dug down" to prevent animals from getting into her chicken coop

          until her fingers were raw. In paragraph 19, the text says she worked

(C2)   through supper and she was "exhausted and her stomach growled."

(E)   From this I can infer that Hattie persevered to make a safe home for her chickens.

Where to Find Evidence in Stories & Literature
Oh, where, oh, where, can we find it?

Evidence can come from . . .	We can find it . . .	We can find it . . .	We can find it . . .
Characters WHO are in the story—children, adults, family, animals, pets, supernatural beings, bugs and odd critters, talking objects	in their **thoughts** *I can think lots of thoughts!*	in their **words** *I can say lots with words!*	• in their **actions** (what they do, how they act) • in their **reactions** (what they do, how they act in response to something) • in their **interactions** (what they do, how they act with others)
Events WHAT happens in the story	in the **beginning**	in the **middle**	at the **end**
Plot HOW a problem or conflict begins, rises, and ends—and its outcome	in the **problem**	as the **action rises**	in the **solution** and **takeaway** (lesson, change)
Author's Use of Craft & Technique (Writers write wisely!)	**in figurative language** • similes • metaphors • personification • and more Stir your language to stir your reader!	**in point of view** • bird's-eye view • first-person point of view • third-person point of view WHO tells the story?	**in tone, mood** For example: *It was a dark and stormy night . . .*
Other STUFF!	**in notes before and after text** *Dear Reader, Before you read this, you'll want to know . . .* *Dear Reader, Now that you've read this, you'll want to know . . .*	**in visuals, graphics, and special features** • pictures/illustrations • photographs • graphics = speech balloons, captions, and so on • and more	**in the layout** How things look on a page (use of space, fonts, and presentation)

Where to Find Evidence in Articles & Informational Texts

Text details	Who, what, when, where, why, and how
Visuals and captions	Charts, graphs, diagrams, photographs, maps, captions
Structure/ organization	<ul><li>The way the introduction, body, and conclusion paragraphs forge an author's central message</li><li>The way in which the information is presented—sequence, comparison, cause/effect, problem/solution</li></ul>
Text features	The use of headings, subheadings, sidebars, index, glossary, reader notes, and so on
Technique	An author's use of expository technique, such as questioning, interview, point of view, figurative language

Think & Discuss: How to Use Evidence

1. Use the author's words in a **quote** or **quotation**.

- Quote a complete sentence.
  "Humpty Dumpty sat on a wall."

- Quote four or five words or a phrase.
  He "sat on a wall."

- Quote one keyword.
  Humpty had a "great" fall.

How to use a quote as evidence in your answer:

- Select what and how much you want to quote. (Don't overuse the author's words and ideas. Yours are also important!)

- Copy the words just as they look in the story.

- Place quotation marks at the beginning and the end of the quote.

2. Use your own words to **sum up** (or **summarize**) main ideas or critical events.

Humpty fell off of the wall.

3. Use your own words to **retell** (or **paraphrase**) main ideas in an article or events in a story.

Once there was an egg named Humpty Dumpty. He climbed a wall and sat at the top. Sadly, he fell, broke, and couldn't be fixed by the King's men and horses.

How to use a summary or a retelling/ paraphrase in your answer:

- Select what and how much you want to sum up or retell/paraphrase. (Don't retell details that aren't useful for your evidence.)

- Use your own words to tell the author's ideas.

- A summary tells parts of the text, and a retelling/paraphrase tells all.

Think & Discuss: Transition Words for Short Response

Connectors (words to connect your details)	**Starters** (words to begin your details)
• Next, . . . • Also, . . . • Additionally, . . . • Second, . . . • Furthermore, . . . • Another example . . .	• I know this because . . . • According to the text, . . . • From the reading, I know that . . . • The author says . . . • The text shows . . . • Proof of this is in . . . • Evidence in paragraph X says . . . • As stated in paragraph X, . . . • In paragraph X, the character . . . • The author reveals/explains/expresses/ shows us/notes/describes . . .

Proofread to Perfection Checklist

☐ **1. Plan one more "whisper-read" of your entire response.** Even though you may have reread parts of your "real-time" response as you were writing it, one more read-through after you finish writing might reveal other easy fixes. Whisper-reading helps you hear if your sentences are complete, fluent, and clear. Listen to be sure your ideas come across the way you intended.

☐ **2. Whisper-read with your pencil—point down and on the prowl!** You'll be proofreading and editing at the same time. Small changes become quick fixes if you're ready and set to make changes.

☐ **3. Be on the prowl for errors that could make your meaning unclear.** Use a simple acronym (such as CUPS) to remind you what to look for.

　　C = capitals
　　U = understanding or usage (agreement, tense)
　　P = punctuation
　　S = spelling (including common spelling errors)

☐ **4. RACE Review** Check that you have restated and answered the question, cited evidence, and edited your response.

☐ **5. Do the last-but-not-least handwriting sweep!** Tidy up letter formation, spacing, and placement on the lines as needed.

CUPS Checklist

☐ **Capitals**
　Check for capitals at the beginning of a sentence, proper nouns, MINTS (months, the letter *I*, names, titles, start of sentences)

☐ **Understanding**
　Whisper-read sentences to helps you listen to your ideas and check for:

　● agreement

　● tense

　● pronoun

　● a clumsy-sounding sentence for a variety of reasons

☐ **Punctuation**

　● punctuation at the end of sentences

　● correct use of commas

☐ **Spelling**

RACE Real-Time Planner

R = restate
A = answer
C = cite evidence
E = edit

I (introduction)[1]	
RA #1 (restate/answer)	**C1** (cite evidence) **C2**
RA #2	**C1** **C2**
RA #3	**C1** **C2**
C (conclusion)[2]	
E (edit)	

[1]The *I* serves as a placeholder/reminder for an introduction. It will be written using words from the task (Lesson 16).
[2]The *C* serves as a placeholder/reminder for a conclusion. It will be based on the introduction (Lesson 16).

31 "Humpty Dumpty" and "Little Boy Blue" are children's nursery rhymes that were written long ago. Nursery rhymes are simple stories that were often used to teach young children lessons. What is a lesson that "Humpty Dumpty" and "Little Boy Blue" teach children? How does each story teach that lesson? Use details from both stories to support your response.

In your response, be sure to:

- describe a lesson that both stories teach.

- explain how the lesson is taught in both stories.

- use details from both stories.

You may plan your writing for question 31 on the blank page provided (not shown).

Humpty Dumpty

Humpty Dumpty sat on a wall.
Humpty Dumpty had a great fall.
All the King's horses and all the King's men
Couldn't put Humpty Dumpty together again.

Little Boy Blue

Little Boy Blue, come blow your horn!
The sheep's in the meadow,
The cow's in the corn.
Where is that boy who looks after the sheep?
He's under a haystack, fast asleep.

It Came From the Mud

A little brown fish swims in the shallow water by the muddy seashore. It's a mudskipper! As the fish swims, the water slowly pulls back from the shore. Now it's low tide. The mudskipper is left on the shore. For most fish, being left on land would be a big problem. But it's not a problem for the mudskipper.

Most fish need to stay underwater to survive, but the mudskipper is different. It is an **amphibious** fish. That means it can live in water or on land! Its body parts help it live in both places.

Fantastic Fins and Tails

Most fish have fins and tails to swim in the water. Mudskippers do too.

But the mudskipper also uses these body parts to move on land. How? It lies on its belly on the mud. It reaches forward with its fins. Then it drags itself along the muddy shore on its belly. It can crawl really fast!

The mudskipper uses its tail to jump across the beach. First, it curls its tail. Then it straightens its body and pushes off the ground. Up it goes!

Great Gills and Damp Skin

All fish need oxygen to breathe. But most fish do not have lungs. They use their **gills** to get oxygen from the water. Mudskippers use gills to breathe in the water too. They do not have lungs.

But the mudskipper's body lets it breathe on land too. The mudskipper has little pockets near its gills. When it's swimming, it fills the pockets with water. Then, when it's on land, it gets oxygen from the water in the pockets. It can breathe just fine!

The fish has one more way to breathe on land. It can breathe through its damp skin to get oxygen straight from the air.

Shovel Mouth

All fish have mouths for eating. Mudskippers do too. But mudskippers also use their mouths to build a home for their eggs.

Fish eggs need to be moist to survive. A father mudskipper uses his mouth to dig a burrow. He digs out a mouthful of mud from the seashore. Then he spits it away. He does this again and again to make the burrow longer and deeper. He builds the burrow close to the ocean so that it fills with water.

The mother mudskipper lays her eggs in the burrow. The eggs are safe—and wet—inside the burrow that the dad made with his mouth.

A mudskipper has the same parts as other fish. But it uses them in unusual ways. That's how it survives in the land and water of its seashore home!

Strange Fish

Believe it or not, **seahorses** are fish! They use their long, horse-like snouts to suck up tiny shrimp to eat. They grab onto plants with their long tails.

Flying fish have a tricky way to escape predators in the ocean. They wave their tails to jump out of the water. Then they hold out their fins to glide in the air!

An **archerfish** is a great hunter. It sees a bug on a leaf over the water. The fish spits out a mouthful of water at the bug and knocks it down. Then the fish eats the bug!

32 Scientists who study fish and mammals explain that they look the way they do often because their survival depends on it. In other words, these creatures may have special, easy-to-see features that help them survive in their environments. Write an essay that explains the features that some fish and mammals have that help them survive. Be sure to use facts and details from both passages to support your explanation.

Be sure to include:

- an introduction
- support for your ideas using information from the passages
- a conclusion that is relevant

Your response should be in the form of a multiple-paragraph essay. You may plan your writing for question 32 on the blank page provided (not shown).

Tricky Words/Phrases Used in Short- and Extended-Response Questions

Word/Phrase	Swap Words (synonyms, similar meanings)
Contribute to	help, support, add value to, strengthen, add to
Best support	show, prove, strengthen, shore up
Show	tell us, prove, make us aware of
Reveal	show, tell, make aware, clear up
Suggest	mean, show us, tell us, make us think
Express	tell, say, inform
State	say, tell, show
Relate to	connect
Add to a reader's understanding	show, strengthen, build
Connect to	relate
Conclude	tell, discover, learn, find out, sum up
Alike	the same, similar, share characteristics
Similar	alike, the same, share characteristics
Compare	notice how things are alike, similar, the same
Contrast	notice how things are different, not the same, dissimilar
Affect	impact, change, cause
Challenge	problem, conflict, obstacle
Refer to	talk about, name, bring up
Word, phrase, sentence, quote, simile, article, story, illustrations, maps, photographs, subheadings	features found in text passages
Paragraph	sentences grouped together and contributing to an idea
Excerpt	section of a text (beginning, middle, or end) which may include additional reader notes to explain the context
Main idea, theme, claim	critical idea in a passage

How to Use Evidence in Extended-Response Tasks

Balance evidence with original thinking 	Make sure your own ideas are in the answer: • You can share your inference (Lesson 10) to answer the question. • You can explain how the author's words support your ideas.
Weigh evidence. 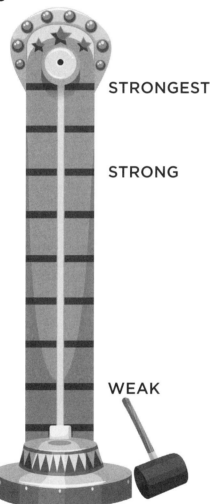 STRONGEST STRONG WEAK	Make sure your evidence is the BEST it can be. • You can use the best example by selecting the strongest first. **Strongest example** • right on target • emphasized in the passage • easy to find • easy to explain how it supports your ideas **Strong example** • mostly on target • receives good coverage in the passage • may be repeated/supported elsewhere in the passage • mostly easy to find • mostly easy to explain how it supports your idea **Weak example** • not really on target (doesn't clearly support your idea—it's a stretch) • receives little coverage in the passage • isn't repeated or supported elsewhere in the passage • difficult to find • difficult to explain how it supports your idea Using two or three details to support your idea may mean that some evidence isn't as strong as you might like. You can often make it stronger if you combine details (use two together as a single piece of evidence) or when you explain how the evidence supports your idea (a rich, detailed explanation).
Spread the evidence so <u>all</u> questions in the task are strong. 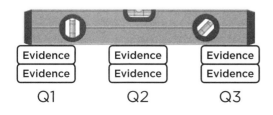	Make sure you have two or three pieces of evidence in your RACE Real-Time Planner for all questions in the task. This should help you address each question evenly. Avoid uneven discussion or explanation in your responses.

Writing From a Planner: Sentence Rehearsals

Introduction	**Include . . .** **1.** Title **2.** Author **3.** Keywords from task
Body Paragraphs **Trial 1 = In-Your Head Sentence** Say your sentence in your head or whisper-read your sentence. — Fix-Up #1 — **Trial 2 = Say & Write Sentence** Say your new sentence in your head as you write it down. — Fix-Up #2 — **Trial 3 = Reread/Rewrite Sentence** Read your written sentence in your head. — Fix-Up #3 —	**Trials** Fix-Up #3 Trial 3 Fix-Up #2 Trial 2 Fix-Up #1 Trial 1
Conclusion	**Include . . .** **1.** Title **2.** Keywords **3.** Takeaway idea (linked to theme/main idea)

Typical Fix-Ups:
- Frame the idea in a complete sentence.
- Make choppy sentences flow smoothly.
- Check details, quotes, and spelling by flipping back to the passage.
- Strengthen short, weak wording.
- Shorten long, run-on wording.

More Transitions & Transitional Phrases

As you revise and edit with CRAFT, you can improve the transitions in your extended response. Remember, transitions help our writing flow. They also guide our readers through our writing! Here's some kicked-up CRAFT transitions.

CRAFT Evidence Starters

- I can support my ideas because . . .
- After close reading the text, it's clear that . . .
- As evidence, the text states . . .
- As evidence, the author includes the details . . .
- My inference makes sense because . . .
- Although the author doesn't state this outright, it's easy to infer that . . .
- (event), proving/confirming/explaining . . .
- (event), suggesting/causing me to believe that/leading me to think . . .

CRAFT Evidence Additions (weighted for meaning)

- In addition to (description of earlier example), another example proves . . .
- Adding to (description of earlier example), another example shows . . .
- While (description of earlier example), other evidence strengthens the claim that . . .
- Moreover, the evidence in paragraph X strongly supports the claim that . . .
- A similar piece of evidence is shown in . . .
- A different form of evidence is shown in . . .
- Unlike this first piece of evidence, another . . .
- A better piece of evidence is . . .
- Stronger evidence is shown in paragraph X, where . . .
- Of equal importance, the text states that . . .
- Of greater significance, . . .

Concluding a Claim

- There is no doubt that . . .
- Without question . . .
- This collection of evidence suggests . . .
- This strong evidence shows . . .

Routine Response Writing Prompt

Title: _____ Date: _____

Some prompts for your Writer's Response Journal:

1. What was going through your mind as you read this?

2. How did you feel while reading this part?

3. What questions did you have when you finished reading?

4. What do you think are the one or two most important ideas in the text?

5. What will you remember most about this text?

6. What would you do if this happened to you?

My response to today's reading:

_____

_____

_____

_____

_____

_____

_____

_____

_____

_____

_____

_____

_____

What's My Text-Marking Style?

How much and what kind of text-marking is right for me? Take this survey to find out.

1. Does my text-marking help me quickly find what I'm looking for in the passage? Place an X on the scale.

Usually		Sometimes		Always
☐ 1	☐ 2	☐ 3	☐ 4	☐ 5

2. How much text-marking works best for me? Place an X on the scale.

Usually		Sometimes		Always
☐ 1	☐ 2	☐ 3	☐ 4	☐ 5

3. Do I like to mix and match my text-marking methods? Circle the ones you use most often.

Underline   **Gist statements**   **Hashtags**

4. Based on my answers above, are there any changes I can make to improve my text-marking style?

_____

_____

5. Are there other ways I text-mark that are unique to my style?

_____

_____

What's My Planning Style?

How much planning for my written responses is right for me?
Take this survey to find out.

1. Does my planning help me write my response? Can I follow my plan easily
   and does it simplify my work? Place an X on the scale.

Usually		Sometimes		Always
☐ 1	☐ 2	☐ 3	☐ 4	☐ 5

2. How many notes do I like to include in my planner? Place an X on the scale.

A little		Average		A lot
☐ 1	☐ 2	☐ 3	☐ 4	☐ 5

3. Do I like to use symbols (e.g., letters for names) or other codes in my plans
   (e.g., color-coding or coding the details I'll use as evidence)?
   Circle the one(s) you use most often.

Symbols   **Code the text**

4. Based on my answers above, are there any changes I can make to improve my planning?

_____

_____

5. Are there other ways I plan that are unique to my style?

_____

_____

Am I Taking Charge of My Answers?

Are your good ideas—instead of a formula—shaping your answer?
Take this survey to find out.

1. Do I start my answer in a way that makes sense to me? Place an X on the scale.

Usually		Sometimes		Always
☐ **1**	☐ **2**	☐ **3**	☐ **4**	☐ **5**

2. Do I support my ideas in a way that makes sense to me? Place an X on the scale.

Usually		Sometimes		Always
☐ **1**	☐ **2**	☐ **3**	☐ **4**	☐ **5**

3. Do I conclude my answer in a way that makes sense to me? Place an X on the scale.

Usually		Sometimes		Always
☐ **1**	☐ **2**	☐ **3**	☐ **4**	☐ **5**

4. Based on my answers above, are there any changes I can make to improve my take-charge action?

5. Are there other ways I take charge of the formulas (RACE and others) that show my unique style?

Creative Writing Techniques

Technique	Definition	Example
Figurative Language		
Simile	Compares two things using *like* or *as*	
Metaphor	Compares two things without using *like* or *as*	
Personification	Gives nonhuman objects traits of a person	
Idiom	A word or phrase that means something other than what it says	
Imagery		
Sensory details	Details that help readers see, feel, smell, taste, and/or hear	
Sound Techniques		
Interjections	A word or phrase that expresses a feeling	
Onomatopoeia	Using a word that sounds like the noise it makes	
Sentence Structure		
Combine sentences	Turn two short sentences into a longer one	
Change sentence beginnings	Change the order of words to begin a sentence	

Response-Writing Voice Checklist

Does your voice come through in your writing? Use this checklist to find out.

☐ **I have included all "must-haves" in my response.**

> ☐ My introduction includes the title(s), author(s), and keywords from the task.

> ☐ My conclusion includes the title(s), author(s), keywords from the task, and a meaningful takeaway.

☐ **I show that I have connected with the ideas in the passage.** I understand the ideas, I can link them to something I know that matters to me, and I can share my thoughts and feelings about the ideas.

> ☐ I write what I know.

> ☐ I write what I think and feel.

> ☐ I write it in my own way and using my own words by making choices.

> ☐ I write with confidence.

☐ **I show that the ideas in the reading have impacted me.** I have learned something new or I have proven something I already knew, and I can share my thoughts and feelings about the ideas.

> ☐ I write what I know.

> ☐ I write what I think and feel.

> ☐ I write it my own way and using my own words by making choices.

> ☐ I write with confidence.

☐ **My response-writing voice is Can-Do-It-My-Way Confident!**

Online Resources

To download the following resources, go to **www.scholastic.com/closereadingandwriting**.
Enter your email and this code: **SC818834**.

Lesson/Close-Up	Title	Strategy
n/a	Lesson Presentation	n/a
Lesson 5 Close-Up #1	"Picnic Tricks"	underlining and coding
Lesson 5 Close-Up #2	"When Looks Matter"	underlining and coding
Lesson 6 Close-Up #1	"Picnic Tricks"	symbols and more codes
Lesson 6 Close-Up #2	"When Looks Matter"	symbols and more codes
Lesson 7 Close-Up #1	"Picnic Tricks"	gist statements
Lesson 7 Close-Up #1	"Picnic Tricks"	hashtags
Lesson 7 Close-Up #2	"When Looks Matter"	gist statements
Lesson 7 Close-Up #2	"When Looks Matter"	hashtags
Lesson 8 Close-Up #1	"Humpty Dumpty" question #1	RACE (short response)
Lesson 8 Close-Up #2	"An Extreme Adventure"	text-marking
Lesson 8 Close-Up #2	"An Extreme Adventure" question #1	RACE (short response)
Lesson 9 Close-Up #1	"Humpty Dumpty" question #2	Question-Attack & RACE (short response)
Lesson 9 Close-Up #2	"An Extreme Adventure" question #2	Question-Attack & RACE (short response)
Lesson 10 Close-Up #1	"Little Boy Blue" Nailed It! graphic organizers	making inferences (short response)
Lesson 10 Close-Up #2	"An Extreme Adventure" question #3	making inferences (short response)
Lesson 12 Close-Up #1	"Humpty Dumpty" question #2	editing for CUPS
Lesson 12 Close-Up #2	"An Extreme Adventure" question #2	editing for CUPS
Lesson 13 Close-Up #1	"Humpty Dumpty" and "Little Boy Blue" question #31	RACE Real-Time Planner (extended response)
Lesson 13 Close-Up #2	"When Looks Matter" and "It Came From the Mud" question #32	RACE Real-Time Planner (extended response)
Lesson 16 Close-Up #1	"Humpty Dumpty" and "Little Boy Blue" question #31	writing from RACE planner (extended response)
Lesson 16 Close-Up #2	"When Looks Matter" and "It Came From the Mud" question #32	writing from RACE planner (extended response)
Lesson 17 Close-Up #1	"Humpty Dumpty" and "Little Boy Blue" question #31	revising and editing for CRAFT
Lesson 17 Close-Up #2	"When Looks Matter" and "It Came From the Mud" question #32	revising and editing for CRAFT
Lesson 18 Close-Up #1	"Picnic Tricks"	Stray & Play (text-marking)
Lesson 18 Close-Up #2	"Humpty Dumpty" and "Little Boy Blue" question #31	Stray & Play (planning)
Lesson 18 Close-Up #3	"An Extreme Adventure" question #3	Stray & Play (flexible formula)
Lesson 18 Close-Up #4	*The Wizard of Oz* question #30	Stray & Play (paragraphing style)
Lesson 19 Close-Up #1	"Humpty Dumpty" and "Little Boy Blue" question #31	Add More & Explore
Lesson 19 Close-Up #2	"When Looks Matter" and "It Came From the Mud" question #32	Add More & Explore
Lesson 20 Close-Up #1	"Humpty Dumpty" and "Little Boy Blue" question #31	Develop Voice
Lesson 20 Close-Up #2	"When Looks Matter" and "It Came From the Mud" question #32	Develop Voice